DARK PSYCHOLOGY

Learn the Practical Uses and Defenses of Manipulation, Emotional Influence, Persuasion, Deception, Mind Control, Covert NLP, Brainwashing, and Other Secret Techniques

VICTOR SYKES

Table of Contents

INTRODUCTION

Congratulations on purchasing *Dark Psychology* and thank you for doing so.

The following chapters will discuss dark psychology. This form of psychology and understanding of the human mind can be found all around us. No matter how much we may hope that those around us are good and would never try to harm us, there are still people who are going to use our psyche and our emotions against us. This guidebook is going to go into depth about various dark psychology techniques and can arm you with the understanding to keep dark manipulators from taking advantage of you.

There are many different ways that a dark manipulator can try to take control over your mind and get you to react in a certain manner. They can often get in close with you, befriend you, and get you to act in certain ways. And many times, a rational and even an intelligent person will get caught in the trap, without realizing what is going on until it is too late to do anything about it. This is what makes dark psychology so dangerous and why it is so important to learn the signs and understand the different methods early on.

This guidebook will give you the information and the understanding that you need to recognize and defend against dark psychology. We will discuss some of the different methods that are used with dark psychology, why a dark manipulator will use these techniques, and more to help you understand what signs to look out for.

One of the best things that you can do to protect yourself from dark psychology is to know as much about it as possible. Take a look through this book and learn the main types of psychology that are out there that fit into this realm of darkness and manipulation.

There are plenty of books on this subject on the market. Thanks again for choosing this one! Every effort was made to ensure it is full of as much useful information as possible. Please enjoy!

BONUS!

As an additional 'thank you' for reading this book, I want to give you another book for free. The book is:

The Simple and Powerful Word To Use to Increase Your Social Status

It's a quick read that will add a powerful tool to your psychological toolbox.

Follow the link below and you can claim the book instantly.

Click Here for Instant Access!

or go to VictorSykes.com/free-ebook

CHAPTER 1:

What s Dark Psychology?

Before we take a look at some of the methods that come with dark psychology and how it can be used against you, it is important to know exactly what this form of psychology is about. Psychology, or an understanding of how the human mind works, is a part of all of our lives. Psychology is going to underpin everything in our lives from advertising to finance, crime to religion, and even from hate to love. Someone who is able to understand these psychological principles is someone who really holds onto the key to human influence.

This is not an easy task, which is why most people don't possess it. Learning all of the different principles of psychology is not necessary. Start with the lessons in these pages, and you'll have a solid foundation. You have to be able to read people, understand what makes them tick, and understand why they may react in ways that may not be normally expected. And even then, you may need to spend time taking classes and reading through countless books to gain a complete understanding. It depends how far you want to go with this.

So, if only a few people really understand psychology and how the human mind works, why is it so important to know what this is? It is because those who do know what it is and how to use it can choose to use that power and that knowledge against you.

Dark psychology is going to be any type of deviant or criminal behaviors that are committed against others, usually innocent victims. The one using dark psychology is going to prey on someone who they see as weaker or vulnerable. This doesn't mean they are actually weak, but they can be easily influenced or easily read for the benefit of the manipulator.

Dark psychology is always present in the world. There are always those who will search for the weaknesses in others, in order to benefit themselves. They will use lying, withholding of love, persuasion, and manipulation in order to get what they want. And they are often successful at it because they can easily read the person they are trying to target.

Many people live in denial. They assume that dark psychology is not there and that it is not really a problem they need to deal with. But thinking that this type of psychology isn't even there is a bad choice. You can choose to remain ignorant of this, or you can learn how to take control so that you can protect yourself and others from those who would like to cause you harm or ruin you.

Being able to understand dark psychology is not just a defensive measure. There are a lot of principles and ideas found within the world of dark psychology. And simply by knowing them, you will be able to be on the lookout for someone using these techniques. This kind of knowledge is going to be useful whenever someone tries to use those techniques against you.

Once you have pulled back the curtain of the world of dark psychology, you will find that there is so much more to human nature than you ever imagined. Let's take a look at how this can work.

How Is Dark Psychology Used Today?

While some people are going to use these dark psychology tactics in order to harm their victim, there are times when you may use these tactics without the intent of negatively manipulating another person. Some of these tactics were either unintentionally or intentionally added to our toolbox from a variety of means that could include:

- When you were a child, you would see how adults, especially those close to you, behaved.

- When you were a teenager, the mind and your ability to truly understand the behaviors around you were expanded.

- You were able to watch others use the tactics and then succeed.

- Using the tactics may have been unintentional in the beginning, but when you found that it worked to get you what you wanted, you would start to use those tactics in an intentional manner.

- Some people, such as a politician, a public speaker, or a salesperson, would be trained to use these types of tactics to get what they want.

Dark Psychology Tactics That Are Used on a Regular Basis

- Love flooding: This would include any buttering up, praising, or complimenting people to get them to comply with the request that you want. If you want someone to help you move some items into your home, you may use love flooding in order to make them feel good, which could make it more likely that they will help you. A dark manipulator could also use it to make the other person feel attached to them and then get them to do things that they may not normally do.

- Lying: This would include telling the victim an untrue version of the situation. It can also include a partial truth or exaggerations with the goal of getting what you wanted to be done.

- Love denial: This one can be hard on the victim because it can make them feel lost and abandoned by the manipulator. This one basically includes withholding affection and love until you are able to get what you want out of the victim.

- Withdrawal: This would be when the victim is given the silent treatment or is avoided until they meet the needs of the other person.

- Restricting choices: The manipulator may give their victim access to some choices, but they do this in order to distract them from the choices that they don't want the victim to make.

- Semantic manipulation: This is a technique where the manipulator is going to use some commonly known words, ones that have accepted meanings by both parties, in a conversation. But then they will tell the victim, later on, that they had meant something completely different when they used that word. The new meaning is often going to change up the entire definition and could make it so that the conversation goes the way the manipulator wanted, even though the victim was tricked.

- Reverse psychology: This is when you tell someone to do something in one manner, knowing that they will do the opposite. But the opposite action is what the manipulator wanted to happen in the first place.

Who Will Deliberately Use Dark Tactics?

There are many different people who may choose to use these dark tactics against you. They can be found in many different aspects of your life, which is why it is so important to learn how to stay away from them. Some of the people who are able to use some of these dark psychology tactics deliberately include:

- Narcissists: These individuals are going to have a bloated sense of their own self-worth, and they will have the need to make others believe that they are superior as well. In order to meet their desires of being worshipped and adored by everyone they meet, they will use persuasion and dark psychology.

- Sociopaths: Those who are sociopaths are charming, intelligent, and persuasive. But they only act this way to get what they want. They lack any emotions, and they are not able to feel any remorse. This means that they have no issue with using the tactics of dark psychology to get what they want, including taking it as far as creating superficial relationships.

- Politicians: With the help of dark psychology, a politician could convince someone to cast votes for them simply by convincing these people that their point of view is the right one.

- Salespeople: Not all salespeople are going to use dark tactics against you. But it is possible that some, especially those who are really into getting their sales numbers and being the best, will not think twice about using dark persuasion in order to manipulate people.

- Leaders: Throughout history, there have been plenty of leaders who will use the techniques of dark psychology in order to get their team members, subordinates, and citizens do what they want.

- Selfish people: This could be any person that you come across who will make sure that their own needs are put before anyone else's. They aren't concerned about others, and they will let others forego their benefits so that they can benefit. If the situation benefits them, it is fine if it benefits someone else. But if someone is going to be the loser, it will be the other person and not them.

This list is important because it is going to serve two purposes. First, it is going to help you be more aware of the people who may try to manipulate you to do things that you don't want to do, and it can be there to help out with self-realization. Being on the lookout for those who want to get something out of you, without any concerns about how it will affect you, is one of the main goals of this book so that you can arm yourself against dark psychology.

CHAPTER 2:

The Basics of Covert Emotional Manipulation

Covert emotional manipulation is very important to the art of dark psychology. Many of the tactics that are used with dark psychology are going to use this type of emotional manipulation, whether in part or completely. As you start to learn a bit more about the world of dark psychology and its different manifestations, you will soon start to see the signs of CEM. This is why it is so important to understand what CEM is exactly so that you can watch out for it in your daily life.

Covert emotional manipulation, or CEM, is going to be an attempt by one person to try and influence the feelings and the thoughts of the other person in a way that is considered underhanded and that is undetected by the one who is being manipulated. Being able to break down each of the words that are in CEM is important to help you get a better idea on the foundations of this topic.

Covert refers to the way that a manipulator is able to hide their intentions. They want to be able to hide the true nature of all their actions. Remember that not all types of influence and emotional manipulation will be categorized as covert. The victims of the type that is covert though will typically not realize they are being manipulated and will not be able to understand the way the manipulation is carried out. In some cases, they are not even able to look and figure out the motivation of their manipulator. This is why CEM is such a stealth bomber in the world of dark psychology. Its point is to avoid detection and defense until it is too late for the victim.

The emotional side of the manipulator is going to be the specific focus of that manipulator. Other types of manipulation may include things like the willpower, beliefs, and behaviors of the other person. Many manipulators will focus on this area of influence as they are well aware that the emotions of the other person are key to the other aspects of their personality.

Being able to manipulate the emotions of the other person is key. If a person has emotional control over the other person, then they are going to have full control over them.

The final piece of CEM is manipulation. It is commonly thought that manipulation and influence are the same things. This is not true though. Manipulation is going to refer to the hidden and underhand process of influence that will take place outside the awareness of the one who is being controlled. The intention behind this compared to someone who has the intention to influence can be a big difference.

With an influencer, they are going to go into this with the idea of "I want to help you make a decision that is good for you." But with the manipulator, they have the thoughts of "I want to secretly control you in order to provide benefit to myself." As you can see, both of these are quite a bit different, so understanding the intention behind any given behavior is going to be a large part in deciding whether the situation is covert emotional manipulation or not.

Situation and Manipulations

There are four main scenarios in which CEM is able to take place. These include the family, romantic, personal, and professional parts of your life. One of the most common forms of CEM is romantic, and it can sometimes be the most deadly. There are some less obvious forms of CEM that you are able to find anywhere, and because they are less common, they can sometimes be the most dangerous.

A good example of CEM is a controlling romantic partner. If a woman is in a relationship and her partner is trying to control her, she is going to be disgusted by what is going on, once she figures it out. She may want to find a way to get out of the situation. Because of this, many times the controlling partner is going to exercise their influence as covertly as possible. They don't want their partner to know they are being controlled, or the victim leaves, and there is no one left to control.

If the manipulator is successful, then their wife or their girlfriend will continue to be a victim of emotional manipulation, and they may have a hard time realizing that it is going on. This allows the manipulator to keep the control that they want without any risk of being discovered and losing the other person for good.

This can also happen with a friend who would use CEM in order to get the outcomes they want when they have a relationship with another person. In this group, one of the common types of manipulators is going to be someone who covertly induced feelings of obligation, sympathy, and guilt in a friend. The friend is being manipulated in this way without being aware that they are being influenced. They may realize that they are behaving in a different way to that friend, but they won't be able to explain why and how.

You will find that the professional part of your life can be another place for covert emotional manipulators. There are a lot of people who have worked for a boss or another person who had authority, who seems to trigger some unknown feelings of duty, fear, and guilt in them. People who are manipulated this way may never be able to identify why these feelings exist or where they come from.

And in the world of CEM, the family can be the most problematic. A skilled manipulator is able to find a victim, even within their own family, and the amount of influence that they exercise can be dangerous. This is because the manipulator and the victim will have a very deep connection together because they are related. When blood relations are added in, the amount of influence and control can increase quite a bit.

The reason that these family situations are so suited to using CEM is that most people already feel a level of social obligation in order to help their own family. They are willing to go a little further to ensure the needs of their family are attended to. Because of this predisposition, covert emotional manipulative practices will give you a victim that is very malleable.

CHAPTER 3:

Some Common Covert Manipulation Methods

We have spent some time talking about what covert manipulation is all about and how it can be used to benefit the manipulator. Now it is time to look at a few of the different methods that can be used in covert manipulation. These are meant to bring out feelings of guilt, sadness, or something else. The manipulator also wants to make sure that they can do all of this without the victim detecting them if at all possible. Let's take a look at some of the techniques that are used by people practicing CEM.

Love Bombing

Love bombing is a technique that many emotional manipulators will use when they get started with their interactions with their victim. It is going to involve an intense, sudden, and forceful display of lots of positive feelings to a victim. This may seem a bit counterintuitive in the beginning when we are talking about CEM. If the manipulator is trying to cause harm to someone, why would they work to intensify the positivity in the beginning? It's because doing this can serve their own objectives.

The idea behind working with love bombing is that it is going to create an intense feeling of affection, trust, and compliance from the victim over to their manipulator. The extent of which love bombing is going to be used, and the person it is used on, will often depend on how the manipulator assesses the situation. A victim who seems lonely, seeking support, comfort, and desperate is more likely to be love bombed and at a higher intensity than others. If the victim is more grounded, then they will need a less intense, and maybe more subtle, way in the love bombing.

Reinforcement: A CEM Stacked Sequence

After the love bombing, a pattern of intermittent positive reinforcement is going to show up. This is a way of controlling the victim without them really knowing what is going on. The typical sequence of a CEM scenario is going to involve love bombing, then positive reinforcement, and then intermittent positive reinforcement. Let's take a look at how this is done and how it benefits the manipulator.

Love bombing is going to be the unconditional, unearned, and intense display of positivity that comes from a manipulator to their target. This is going to happen right when the two meet and start interacting with each other. The purpose of this is to help soften up the defenses of the victim and can make the victim more reliant on the person who is manipulating them. This helps set the frame of a positive friendship, relationship, or another form that this interaction takes.

After love bombing has occurred early in the relationship, it is time for the manipulator to move over to positive reinforcement. This is when the manipulator is going to switch their behavior, and they will no longer show unconditional positivity to the victim. Instead, the manipulator is going to withhold any positivity until the victim is performing the behavior that they desire.

A good example of this is when the manipulator wants to make sure that the victim calls them on a regular basis. The manipulator is only going to show a positive response when the victim does this. If the manipulator does this in a positive way, then the victim will be unaware that this positive attention is being used in a strategic manner against them. They will simply start to comply with the wishes of the manipulator because they want to experience those good feelings again.

This type of predictable positive reinforcement, after it has been used for some time, is going to then be replaced by Intermittent Positive Reinforcement, which is also known as IPR. This IPR is going to involve withholding of expressions of positivity, even when the desired behavior is displayed. For example, let's say that the manipulator wants their victim to offer to purchase them things. And when the victim complies, the manipulator is going to only reward this behavior with their positive response on occasion, and not all the time.

This type of unpredictability is going to cause a deep, subconscious craving for the victim to want more positive attention. But the victim won't even realize what is going on. They will chase that good reaction from the manipulator using any means that they can. The manipulator is going to win because they have their victim behaving in a specific way, and the victim will not really have an awareness of what they are doing or why they are doing it.

Reality Denial

One of the most terrifying things that a human can endure is the feeling that they are losing their own sanity. This is bad enough if it is explained by something that the victim can understand, such as a byproduct of stress in their lives. But this can be really unsettling if this insanity feeling is induced by the emotional manipulator.

Reality denial is going to refer to a range of techniques used in CEM that have the purpose of destroying the sanity of the victim in order to serve the selfish aims. The ways that this takes place, and its impact, will vary based on the method that works the best for the manipulator.

One of the main ideas of reality denial is that it happens gradually. If the manipulator tries to do it all at once, the victim is going to notice and will stay away. Because of this, the manipulator is unlikely to instantly aim to destroy the sanity of their victim right away. This type of outcome is almost impossible for you to achieve without being detected.

Instead of doing this, a skilled manipulator is going to take a slower but steady approach. This means they are going to slowly erode at the sanity of the other person until that victim isn't able to trust their own faculties. But how does the manipulator turn this reality denial process on? It is often going to start with a small-scale undermining of the confidence of a victim in their own memory. The manipulator will then be able to engineer various situations where the victim will feel like they need to question their own recollection of events. They won't know what is true and what isn't any longer.

Of course, during this process, the manipulator is going to ensure that the portrayal of what really happened is the one that seems the most credible to their victim.

This process of slowly eroding the confidence of the victim is going to serve two purposes to the manipulator. First, it is going to reduce the amount of trust the victim has in their own powers of understanding and recall. Second, this trust will then be moved over to the manipulator.

One thing to remember is that this transference of trust is never going to be that big of a deal in the transaction, especially in the beginning. When the manipulator gets started, it is simply going to look like they are the one who has a slightly better memory than the victim. The victim may even be thankful that they have someone around whose recollection they are actually able to rely on, rather than seeing this as a form of manipulation that is being used against them by the manipulator.

Of course, this is going to start increasing over time as well. The covert emotional manipulator is going to start increasing the severity of the events that they want the victim to question. What may seem like a harmless and even insignificant situation, in the beginning, is going to amplify. It will eventually reach the point where the victim seems to lose all their own confidence in their cognitive powers and will question their own sanity.

The part of this process that seems the most insidious most of the time is the fact that the victim is often going to start blaming their own mind for losing these abilities. A skilled manipulator is not going to be seen as the one who is pulling strings. Even though they are in charge of this slow demise in the sanity, they will never let their victim know what is going on behind the scenes.

These different methods can often be used together. But the key is that they need to be done covertly. If the victim realizes what is going on, they will walk away and refuse to be influenced by the manipulator. But skilled manipulators are able to use the different techniques above in order to get the victim to behave in a certain way, and the victim usually doesn't realize what is going on or why they feel a certain way.

CHAPTER 4:

Dark Persuasion

Persuasion is an interesting topic. There are lots of persuasions that are considered just fine in society. They are acceptable, and even some people hold jobs where they will spend a lot of time trying to persuade others. Any attempt by one person to influence someone else to do some action can be persuasion. A salesperson at a car dealership is using persuasion because they try to persuade someone to purchase a new vehicle. This isn't seen as something sinister or bad. The difference here is that this persuasion and other similar examples of persuasion benefit both parties. The car dealer makes a sale and some money, and the "victim" is going to get a new vehicle.

There are a lot of legitimate types of persuasion that aren't considered part of dark psychology. The car dealer above is an example. If a negotiator uses their skills to persuade a terrorist to let their hostage go, this is a good form of persuasion. If you convince someone to come along to an event that they will enjoy, then this is a good form of persuasion. This type of persuasion is seen as positive persuasion. But then, what would count as dark persuasion?

Understanding Dark Persuasion

The first difference you will notice between positive and dark persuasion is the motive behind it. Positive persuasion is used in order to encourage someone to complete an action that isn't going to cause them any harm. In some cases, such as with the negotiator saving a hostage, this persuasion can be used to help save lives.

But with dark persuasion, there isn't really any form of moral motive. The motive is usually amoral, and often immoral. If positive persuasion is understood as a way to help people help themselves, then dark persuasion is more of the process of making people act against their own self-interest. Sometimes, people are going to do these actions begrudgingly, knowing that they are probably not making the right choice, but they do it because they are eager to stop the incessant persuasion efforts. In other cases, the best dark persuader is going to make their victim think that they acted wisely, but the victim is actually doing the opposite in that case.

So, what are the motivations for someone who is a dark persuader? This is going to depend on the situation and the individual who is doing the persuading. Some people like to persuade their victims in order to serve their own self-interests. Others are going to act through with the intention just to cause some harm to the other person. In some cases, the persuader is not going to really benefit from darkly persuading their victim, but they do so because they want to inflict pain on the other person. And still, others enjoy the control that this kind of persuasion gives to them.

You will also find that the outcome you get from dark persuasion is going to differ from what happens with positive persuasion. With positive persuasion, you are going to get one of three scenarios including the following:

- The benefit goes to the person who is being persuaded.

- There is a win/win benefit for the persuaded and the persuader.
- There is a mutual benefit for the person who is persuaded and a third party.

All of these outcomes are good because they will involve a positive result for the person who is being persuaded. Sometimes, there will be others who benefit from these actions. But out of all three situations, the persuaded party is always going to benefit.

With dark persuasion, the outcome is going to be very different. The persuader is the one who will always benefit when they exercise their need for influence or control. The one who is being persuaded often goes against what is in their self-interest when they listen, and they are not going to benefit from all this dark persuasion.

In addition, the most skilled dark persuaders are not only able to cause some harm to their victims while also benefiting themselves, but they could also end up harming others in the process.

Unmasking the Dark Persuader

At this point, you may be curious about who is using these dark methods of persuasion. Are there actually people out there who are interested in using this kind of persuasion and using it against others to cause harm?

The main characteristics of a dark persuader are either an indifference toward or an inability to care about how persuasion is going to impact others. Such people who use this kind of persuasion are going to be often narcissistic and will see their own needs as more important than the needs of others. They may even be sociopathic and unable to grasp the idea of someone else's emotions.

Many times, this kind of dark persuasion is going to show up in a relationship. Often one but sometimes both partners are going to be inclined towards trying to use dark persuasion on each other. If these attempts are persistent and endure, then this type of relationship is going to be classified as psychologically abusive, and that is not healthy for the victim in that relationship. Often, they will not realize that there is something going on or that they are darkly persuaded until it is too late, and they are stuck there.

There are many examples of using this kind of dark persuasion in a relationship. If one partner stops the other partner from taking a new job opportunity or doesn't allow them to go out with friends, then this could be an example of dark persuasion. The dark persuader will work to convince the victim that they are acting in a way that is best for the relationship. In reality, the victim is going through a process that harms them and the relationship.

CHAPTER 5:

Dark Persuasion Techniques to Be on the Lookout For

After taking a look at the different types of persuasion and what they all mean, you may be able to see why dark persuasion is such a bad thing and can be harmful to the victim. Being able to recognize the different techniques that the manipulator may use can make it easier to understand when it is being used on you.

So, how exactly is a dark persuader able to use this idea in order to carry out their wishes? There are a few different types of tactics that a dark manipulator is going to use, but some of the most common options include:

The Long Con

The first method that we are going to look at is the Long Con. This method is kind of slow and drawn out, but it can be really effective because it takes so long and is hard to recognize or even pinpoint when something went wrong. One of the main reasons that some people have the ability to resist persuasion is because they feel that they are being pressured by the other person, and this can make them back off. If they feel that there is a lack of rapport or trust with the person who is trying to persuade them, they will steer clear as well. The Long Con is so effective because they are able to overcome these main problems and give the persuader exactly what they want.

The Long Con is going to involve the dark persuader to take their time, working to earn the trust of their victim. They are going to take some time to befriend the victim and make sure that their victim trusts and likes them. This is going to be achieved by the persuader with artificial rapport building, which sometimes seems excessive, and other techniques that will help to increase the comfort levels between the persuader and their victim.

As soon as the persuader sees that the victim is properly readied psychologically, the persuader is going to begin their attempts. They may start out with some insincere positive persuasion. The persuader is going to lead their victim into making a choice or doing some action that will actually benefit the persuader. This is going to serve the persuader in two ways. First, the victim starts to become used to persuasion by that persuader. The second is that the victim is going to start making that mental association between a positive outcome and the persuasion.

The Long Con is going to take a long period of time to complete because the persuader doesn't want to make it too obvious what they are doing. An example of this is a victim who is a recently widowed lady who is vulnerable because of her age and from their bereavement. After her loss, a man starts to befriend her. This man may be someone she knows from church or even a relative. He starts to spend more time with her, showing immense kindness and patience, and it doesn't take too long for her guard to drop when he comes around.

Then this man starts to carry out some smaller acts of positive persuasion that we talked about before. He may advise her of a better bank account to use or a better way to reduce any monthly bills. The victim is going to appreciate these efforts and the fact that the man is trying to help her, and she takes the advice.

Over some time, the man then tries to use some dark persuasion. He may try to persuade her to let him invest some of her money. She obliges because of the positive persuasion that was used in the past. Of course, the man is going to work to take everything he can get from her. If the manipulator is skilled enough, she may feel that he actually tried to help her, but the money is lost because he just ran into some bad luck with the investment. This is how far dark persuasion can go.

Graduality

Often when we hear about acts of dark persuasion, it seems impossible and unbelievable. What they fail to realize is that this dark persuasion isn't ever going to be a big or a sudden request that comes out of nowhere. Dark persuasion is more like a staircase. The dark persuader is never going to ask the victim to do something big and dramatic the first time they meet. Instead, they will have the victim take one step at a time.

When the manipulator has the target only go one step at a time, the whole process seems like less of a big deal. Before the victim knows it, they have already gone a long way down, and the persuader isn't likely to let them leave or come back up again.

Let's take an example of how this process is going to look in real life. Let's say that there is a criminal who wanted to make it so that someone else committed the crimes for them. Gang bosses, cult leaders, and even Charles Manson did this exact same thing.

This criminal wouldn't dream of beginning the process by asking their victim to murder for them. This would send out a red flag, and no one in their right minds would willingly go out and kill for someone they barely know. Instead, the criminal would start out by having the victim do something small, like a petty crime, or simply hiding a weapon for them. Something that isn't that big of a deal for the victim, at least in comparison.

Over time, the acts that the manipulator is able to persuade their victim to do will become more severe. And since they did the smaller crimes, the persuader now has the unseen leverage of holding some of those smaller misdeeds over the victim, kind of like for blackmail. Before the victim knows it, they are going to feel like they are in too deep. They will then be persuaded to carry out some of the most shocking crimes. And often, by this point, they will do it because they feel like they have no other choice.

Dark persuaders are going to be experts at using this graduality to help increase the severity of their persuasion over time. They know that no victim would be willing to jump the canyon or do the big crime or misdeed right away. So, the persuader works to build a bridge to get there. By the time the victim sees how far in they are, it is too late to turn back.

Masking the True Intentions

There are different methods that a persuader is able to use dark psychology in order to get the things that they want. Disguising their true desires is very important for them to be successful. The best persuaders can use this approach in a variety of ways, but the method they choose is often going to depend on the victim and the situation.

One principle that is used by a persuader is the idea that many people are going to have a difficult time refusing two requests when they happen in a row. Let's say that the persuader wants to get $200 from the victim, but they do not intend to repay the money. To start, the persuader may begin by saying that they need a loan for the amount of $1000. They may go into some details about the consequences to themselves if the persuader doesn't come up with that kind of money sometime soon.

It may happen that the victim feels some kind of guilt or compassion to the persuader, and they want to help. But $1000 is a lot of money, more than the victim is able to lend. From here, the persuader is going to lessen their request from $1000 down to $200, the amount that they wanted from the beginning. Of course, there is some kind of emotional reason for needing the money, and the victim feels like it is impossible to refuse this second request. They want to help out the persuader, and they feel bad for not giving in to the initial request when they were asked. In the end, the persuader gets the $200 they originally wanted, and the victim is not going to know what has taken place.

Another type of technique that the persuader can use is known as reverse psychology. This can also help to mask the true intentions during the persuasion. Some people have a personality that is known as a boomerang. This means that they will refuse to go in the direction that they are thrown and instead will veer off into different directions.

If the persuader knows someone who is more of a boomerang type, then they are able to identify a key weakness of that person. For example, let's say that a persuader has a friend who is attempting to win over some girl they like. The persuader knows that the friend will use and then hurt that girl. The girl is currently torn between the malicious friend and an innocent third party. The persuader may try to steer the girl in the direction of the guy who is actually a good choice, knowing that she is going to go against this and end up going with the harmful friend.

Leading Questions

Another method of dark persuasion that can be used is known as leading questions. If you have ever had an encounter with a salesman that is skilled, verbal persuasion can be really impactful when it is deployed in careful and calibrated ways. One of the most powerful techniques that can be used verbally is leading questions.

These leading questions are going to be any questions that are intended to trigger a specific response out of the victim. The persuader may ask the target something like "how bad do you think those people are?" This question is going to imply that the people the persuader is asking about are definitely bad to some extent. They could have chosen to ask a question that was non-leading, such as "how do you feel about those people?"

Dark persuaders are masters at using leading questions in a way that is hard to catch. If the victim ever begins to feel that they are being led, then they are going to resist, and it is hard to lead them or persuade them. If a persuader ever senses that their victim starts to catch what is happening, they will quit using that one and switch over to another one. They may come back to that tactic, but only when the victim has quieted down a bit and is more influenceable again.

The Law of State Transference

State is a concept that is going to take a look at the general mood someone is in. If someone is aligned with their deeds, words, and thoughts, then this is an example of a strong and congruent state. The law of state transference is going to involve the concept of someone who holds the balance of power in a situation and can then transfer their emotional state onto the other person they are interacting with. This can be a very powerful tool for the dark persuader to use against their victim.

Initially, the influencer is going to force their own state to match the state that their target naturally has. If the target is sad, and they talk slowly, the influencer is going to make their own state follow this format. The point of this is to create a deep rapport with the target.

After we get to this state match, the influencer is then going to alter their own state subtly and see if they have some compliance for the victim. Perhaps they will choose to speed up their own voice to see if the victim will speed up as well. Once the victim starts to show these signs of compliance, then this is an indication that the influencer is at the hook point.

As soon as this hook point is reached, though it may take some time depending on the target and the situation, then the influencer is going to change their own personal state to the one they want the victim to have. This could be any emotional state that the influencer wants. It could be positive, angry, happy, or indignant. It often depends on what the persuader wants to help reach their goals. This technique is an important one for a dark persuader because it is going to show the impact of subconscious cues on the failure or the success of any type of persuasion.

CHAPTER 6:

Undetected Mind Control

Your mind is your sanctuary. No matter what else can be lost to others, the mind is yours and yours alone. Or so we think. People like to believe that they are the ones in control of their own actions and thoughts. Many times our minds can be susceptible to the influence of others, and this allows others to control our minds if we're not careful.

Think about a time when you watched a horror movie. Your mind and your emotions are already being led and influenced in the movie. All the decisions of the director, from the camera shot, the lighting, and the music can determine how you are going to feel and react. Even though you are in full awareness that you are just watching a movie, the brain is going to respond to the prompts when they are given. If our brain can be so influenced by something that we are aware of, how strong would the influence of a dark manipulator be?

Undetected mind control is often the most deadly type of mind control there is. If someone is already aware that their mind is being influenced, then they have the option to object, either physically, verbally, or mentally. For example, they can choose to avoid any contact with the person who controls them. A lot of people are going to run at the first sign they see of a dangerous person trying to get inside the brain and take over. But if the mind controller is able to get into the brain of their victim without the victim detecting them, then the victim has no chance to put up their defenses before it's too late.

There are going to be two tactics that the manipulator can use to take over the mind of their victim without detection. This includes the use of media and interpersonal interactions. Traditionally, the media mind control was something that was only possible for the larger company. Most individual mind controllers were left to deal with just the interpersonal interactions. But with the changes in technology now, this is no longer the case.

Smartphones and laptops have allowed even individual manipulators to have media mind control. This can make it a very powerful tool that the manipulator can use. While the undetected mind controller is going to be able to use all these methods, they are often going to be more deliberate and only take their actions after some careful consideration. They are sometimes seen as a big more coward compared to some other controllers, such as psychological manipulators, but they will take deliberate actions in order to find the right victim to do the attack on.

Undetected Mind Control Tactics

Now that we know a little bit more about undetected mind control, it is time to learn about some of the methods that are used by manipulators in order to control the mind of a victim in a way that is undetected. We are going to explore both the media and the interpersonal techniques that are in the toolkit of the manipulator. Let's take a look at some of the different undetected mind control tactics.

Finding Those Who Are in Need

The first principle that comes with undetected mind control is to find a victim who has a goal. It has been proven that a person who has a pressing desire or need is someone who will be more susceptible to this type of mind control compared to someone that feels satisfied and at ease. This could range from a small physical goal, such as someone who is thirsty and looking for a drink. Or it can be a more psychological goal, such as someone who is craving affection and love.

A good example of this is the experiment that was conducted to look at subliminal influence or undetected mind control. In this study, there were two sets of people who were shown a film, but this film had a hidden image of iced tea. One set of people in the study were thirsty, and the second group wasn't.

After the movie, when the participants were given the chance to purchase a specific drink from a selection, the ones who were thirsty would purchase the iced tea in greater numbers compared to those who weren't thirsty. This shows that, when the brain is desperate for something, they are gladly taking suggestions on what they should choose.

So, how would you be able to use this principle with an individual on more of an interpersonal level? If the mind controller is able to find a victim who is already craving something in their life, then the manipulator will find that it is easier to control that victim. One example is a victim who just got out of a long-term relationship. They may crave the company again and the mind controller would be able to influence their target into thinking that they are the savior for the victim. In reality, they are going to cause harm and even ruin for the victim, but the victim will crave attention so much that they will fall for the mind control that is put on them.

There are a lot of needs that a manipulator is going to seek in order to exploit their victim including their need for company, their need to belong, and even monetary stability. These vulnerabilities are going to be exploited by someone who is more experienced for a number of purposes. They may want to financially or sexually exploit the victim. They may want to gain the victim's allegiance to form a cult or other extreme movement. Some manipulators just go through this process in order to toy with their chosen victim for their own pleasure.

Restricting Choice

Restricting choice is another form of undetected mind control. It can be a subtle form of this because it is going to provide the manipulator with a range of built-in "get out clauses" if the victim ever starts to get suspicious. The key to this type of mind control is to take away any real choices that the victim has in a specific circumstance, while still providing the illusion that the victim is the one who has the control.

Let's say that there is a woman who is being asked to go out on a date. A regular guy is going to spend some time to ask the question and then stammer out a question that is open-ended. They may say something like "Would you like to go out with me?" This question allows the woman to say yes or no based on their personal preferences. This is the way that people who aren't using manipulation will behave.

But someone who is trying to use mind control will approach all of this in a different way. They will confidently and smoothly work to charm the victim. They will get that person to laugh a bit and lower their guard. Then, with a lot of confidence and assurance, the manipulator will ask something like "So, am I taking you out on Thursday or Saturday?" This limits the choices that the victim can go with. The answer of no really isn't an option here, so the victim will pick one of the dates they are given. The victim can't really say that they weren't in control, but the manipulator had complete control the whole time.

Now, if the manipulator is caught, or the victim realizes that they are limited on the choices they are allowed to make, the manipulator can backtrack and still look innocent. They could say something to their victim like "I can't believe you're analyzing my words so much. That really hurts me and makes me not want to open up to you." This can make the victim feel like they were being mean, and they will likely give in.

Media Control with Images

Just like our five senses can be guides in our lives, they can also be our enemies. Our sense of sight is very powerful. This is why we can even dream visually, even when all the other senses are missing, and we can use our sight in order to see images of past memories. This can make imagery as well as visual manipulation a really powerful technique to use with media mind control.

Because of the changes in technology, impactful imagery techniques are in the hands of manipulators all over the place, and they can even take these techniques and tailor them to their specific victim. So, if their victim seems to have a fear or an aversion to something, the manipulator is able to use the feared images to help access and then warp the emotions of a person without the victim even realizing what's going on.

Let's look at how this type of mind control can work. We are in an age where there are lots of smartphones, videos, and more. Everything is shot in high definition clips and can be sent at fast speeds to someone else. This means that a high-tech manipulator is able to allude to the feared image. For example, if a boyfriend who is manipulative knows that his girlfriend has a big fear of insects, they could "accidentally" put a book with a picture of an insect on its cover in the background somewhere during that video chat. While the girlfriend may not consciously register that the book is there, on an emotional and subtle level, she is going to feel the impact.

Media Mind Control with Sound

Sound is another method that the manipulator can use in order to do mind control. But personal experience and experiments can confirm this. Have you ever had a song that seems to get stuck in your head? How easy did you find it to get that song out of your head? The sound may have had a big influence over yourself, even though you knew it was there.

The power of an audio manipulation is even greater when it is undetected. Experiments have shown that if customers are exposed to music that comes from a specific region, then they are more likely to order wine from that country. When they were questioned about it later, they had no idea that the sound around them was what influenced them for their decision making.

While there are examples with the media mind control with sound in the media and with the government, even individual manipulators are able to use this kind of mind control as well. One of the creepiest forms of this mind control is to subliminally influence the victim when they are asleep. A skilled mind controller can get their victim when that victim is at the most vulnerable, such as when they are sleeping, and then can implant the dark and devious commands in the ear of their victim. This allows the commands to sink into the lowest layers of the brain of that victim.

Another form of this auditory mind control is to mask the words with other words or noises that sound similar. Sounds that are outside the range of human perceptions can be this type of mind control. These sounds will reach a particular frequency, and they can be known to impart a feeling of unease, dread, or terror in those who are unknowingly exposed to them. Once the victim feels scared or trapped, the manipulator can then take control and do what they want from this point.

As you can see, there are a lot of different types of mind control that the manipulator is able to use on their victim. The one they choose will depend on the victim and what the end goal of the manipulator is at the time. The important part is that the manipulator needs to know their victim enough in order to do this type of mind control without worrying that the victim is going to find out what is going on. All of this can come together in order to ensure that the manipulator can get what they want, and the victim often won't realize what is going on until it's too late.

CHAPTER 7:

Dark Psychology and Mind Games

The next topic we can look into is known as mind games. Mind games may be something that you think you understand and are able to recognize in your daily life. And it is probably true that someone has tried to play these games on you, and you were able to catch on to them. However, a true manipulator is able to use these mind games in a way that can build up sympathy for themselves, without the victim ever realizing what is going on.

It is common to attribute a lot of normal behaviors to mind games. If someone is hinting that they have a surprise for you or they are teasing you, you may say that the person is using mind games. In the world of dark psychology, this isn't really true. The intentions of the person who uses genuinely dark mind games are never friendly, positive, or good. Therefore, these innocent games, like surprises and teasing, are going to not fit this category right from the beginning.

If the innocent games that we usually associate with mind games don't fit in this category, then what actually constitutes a mind game? Mind games are going to be any type of psychological scheme on behalf of a manipulator towards their victim. These schemes are intended to play games with the willpower or the sanity of the victim.

This is seen as different from the other forms of manipulation we have discussed because the manipulator is toying with their victim. They probably aren't as invested in how this form of manipulation plays out compared to the other methods, and they don't really care about the severity of the situation.

A dark mind game is often one that the manipulator is just going to play for their delight or their amusement. The manipulator isn't going to have any regard for the wellbeing of the victim. Depending on the type of mind game, the intention will often be to test the victim and explore the psyche all at once. The best mind games here are going to be played without revealing the true nature of the manipulator ever being shown. This can really make it hard to detect the mind game, and it is very destructive once the manipulator decides to employ it.

What is the motivation behind these dark mind games?

The motivation behind the mind game can make the difference in whether it is seen as something positive or if it is part of dark psychology. The range of motivations that come with these manipulative mind games is going to be determined based on what the manipulator wants to do and who their victim is at the time.

One reason that a manipulator may choose to play mind games is to manipulate their chosen victim into performing a specific behavior or getting that victim to feel or think a certain way. The manipulator, with this case, may feel that the other forms of manipulation are not all that effective, and they may try to use something that is less obvious to their target, such as a mind game. The manipulator also has the choice to influence the victim in this way just because it amuses them and not because they are really trying to gain something out of the manipulation.

The specific types of influences that can be gained from playing these types of mind games will be explored here in a bit. But basically, these mind games are useful to a manipulator because they are going to reduce the amount of certainty that the victim has, and the psychological strength that the manipulator gains are very subtle and hard to see. Many times, these mind games are going to be used in a way to achieve influence while maintaining the illusion of autonomy with that victim.

Influencing a victim is not the only motivation behind someone using mind games. Many manipulators will choose to play these mind games just to entertain themselves. They like and get pleasure from plotting out ways to impact the psychology of the victim, and they enjoy watching the victim succumb to their intentions. This is similar to what a sociopath may do. The manipulator is not going to see the other person, their victim, as someone who has feelings and thoughts. Instead, they will see them as a system that is there for the manipulator to learn about and use for fun.

Sometimes the dark mind games are played because they are learned behavior, rather than as a conscious intent by the manipulator. This is when the manipulative individual has been exposed to these mind games throughout the course of their life, and they don't know how to act in any other way. This may seem innocent, but it can be just as dangerous because they learned how to act this way and have developed even more methods to really trick their victims into behaving a certain way.

Some Methods Used in Mind Games

Now that you know a bit more about the differences between regular mind games and dark mind games, it is time to explore the different types of mind games that a manipulator can use. The specific games can sometimes have innocent variants in them, but sometimes these variants are dark. Let's take a look at the different types of mind games that a manipulator may try to employ to get what they want from their victim.

Ultimatums

An ultimatum is when one person is able to present the other with a severe choice. It is often going to take the form of a demand such as "Do this... or this will happen." Some examples of how this may play out include:

- "Lose weight...or I will see other people."
- "Quit smoking...or I will leave you."

Ultimatums are like a request, but it has turned itself more into a demand. They pretty much leave the victim without any choice in the manner. With the example above, the other person will have to lose weight, or they won't be with the person they love any longer. They either need to quit smoking, or the other person is going to leave them. If the victim states that these ultimatums leave them with no choices, the manipulator can always come back and state that the victim had a choice, even though the manipulator knows this isn't true.

There are three factors that are going to determine if the ultimatum is considered dark psychology. First is the type of person who gives the ultimatum, the intention of the other person when giving the ultimatum, and the nature of the request or the ultimatum itself.

First, let's look at the person who is giving the ultimatum. If the ultimatum is a legitimate one, then the person who gives it may have a valid and genuine care about the person they want to help. They may say something like "Lose weight…or you are going to end up with a lot of health problems in the future." There is still an ultimatum because something is going to happen to the victim, but they aren't saying it to be mean or to take away love and care for the other person.

The motivation that comes with that ultimatum is going to be another important element of how you can understand it. Those who issue ultimatums with some good intentions will do it because they want to help make something better in the other person's life. These ultimatums are going to be issues with the intention and the purpose of helping the other person make a good choice and make positive life changes.

Judging the intention of these ultimatums can be difficult, which is sometimes why it is so hard to figure out if the ultimatum is dark or not. But with dark ultimatums, the request is often going to go against what is in the best self-interest of the victim.

The Eternal Breakup

One of the fundamental requirements for a good romantic relationship is that both parties need to have a feeling of contentment and security. People in happy romances or happy marriages are going to feel at ease and will not deal with a constant threat that the relationship is going to end at any time. Masters of manipulation understand these principles and will do everything in their power to invert them. By cultivating a sense of negativity, chaos, and instability in the relationship, the manipulator is able to keep their victim powerless for a long time.

So, what is the eternal breakup is a prolonged and persistent use of threatening to leave someone. This could be a promised, an implied, or an actual breakup that is never followed through on.

With an implied breakup, they will not actually involve the overt mention of the breaking up. Instead, the manipulator is going to hint at the breakup to put some doubt in the mind of their victim. The manipulator may casually mention future plans, ones that don't involve the victim at all. They may even decide to hint at an active breakup by saying something like "Well, I won't put up with that for long" or another veiled hint. Any type of sentence or action that could make the victim doubt if the relationship will last can be counted as an implied breakup.

There is also a promised breakup. This is a step between the two types of breakups. This is going to happen when the manipulator issues a threat to their victim and then overtly states that they intend to break up with their victim in the future. The manipulator may resort to saying something like "I am going to leave you soon, and then I won't have to deal with this anymore." Any instance where the manipulator brings up the idea of a divorce, separation, or breakup, but they don't actually carry out this step is going to be a good example of the promised breakup.

Then there is the actual breakup that never occurs. This is the most severe option with the eternal breakup mind game. This is where the manipulator is actually going to break up with their victim without following through with it. They may decide to pack their bags and leave, recognize that the victim is sad or uncomfortable, and then not follow through with it. They may even break up with the victim, without any intention of following through. They will then "accept" the victim back after the victim shows enough sadness or beginning.

The reason that this tactic works is that the victim has often been used and manipulated by the other partner for some time. They are often vulnerable and susceptible to the influence and the power of the manipulator. This makes them more eager to preserve the relationship, even though it has only a dark psychological playground that is fun for the manipulator but hard on the victim each day. If this type of mind game goes on for a long time, it can result in the victim developing trust issues and other options that are not so good for the health of the victim.

Hard to Get

This is another one that can be part of normal and healthy behavior, but then it can also be a part of dark psychology. An example of a hard to get mind game would be the following: a person wants to seem like they are a bit of a challenge to someone they are interested in. They will decide not to be available all the time. This may involve them not accepting every suggested date, taking their time to reply to calls and messages, and other behaviors. The intention here is to make sure that the other person stays interested, and it can help to give them a happy and healthy relationship together.

But the dark psychological use of hard to get can be a lot more dangerous. Those who use this as a form of manipulation are going to play hard to get games at times other than at the beginning of the relationship. Their intention is not going to lead to a positive situation, and they don't really care at all about the wellbeing of the other person. When this continues onto the later parts of the relationship, it can result in a manipulator in the relationship who is unreliable and very evasive.

There are a lot of different ways that the manipulator can choose to be hard to get outside of the relationship. They may decide to become unavailable or unreliable after the two partners made an agreement to be in a committed relationship. This is an inversion to what is seen in most normal relationships. When you meet someone and decide to be in a relationship with them, this usually means that you are both moving in the right direction and that you become more reliable and available compared to the beginning. This does not happen when a dark manipulator is using the hard to get mind game against one of their victims in a relationship.

With a normal relationship, you will find that things are elusive at the start, but then they become firmer over time. A manipulator is able to artificially make the relationship firm in the beginning. This helps to force a sense of connection with their victim. Then, over time, they are going to become less and less available. This will happen once the victim is hooked and already attached to the manipulator.

When a person decides to play the hard to get mind game later on in the relationship, it is going to put the victim on the defensive, and they will need to put in some extra work. The victim is going to work hard to reconnect with the manipulator, who seems to be pulling away from them.

The point of this is that all this work on the part of the victim is going to gratify the manipulator's ego and can place the power back in their hands. The professional manipulators are able to balance out the actions that make them hard to get with those that convey some reliability and closeness. And when they do this successfully, it is going to lead to a lot of deep psychological confusion and even some instability in the mind of the victim. This allows the manipulator to get in there and exploit the situation in any manner they would like, without the victim realizing.

As you can see, there are many different mind games that a manipulator is able to play against their victim. Depending on the type of relationship that they have with their victim and the end results they are trying to gain, the manipulator can use a combination of these techniques to force the victim to act in the way that they want. This can be really hard on the victim. They often don't realize that they are being used and toyed with until it is too late, and by then they are often so stuck in the situation that they can't really do much about it.

CHAPTER 8:

Understanding Deception

Deception is another key aspect that comes with dark psychology. Like many other tactics that come with dark psychology, it is sometimes difficult to tell whether one instance of deception is considered dark or not. But before we explore more into this, we need to first understand what deception is all about in our world.

Deception is going to be any word or action that is capable of making someone believe something that is not true. Fraudulently providing evidence for something that is false, implying falsehood, omitting the truth, and lying are all examples of deception.

Not all types of deception will count as dark psychology. Everyone is going to deceive others to some extent or another they may deceive others because they feel inadequate, because they feel embarrassed, or even as a kindness. For example, some studies have shown that many men are going to lie about their heights. This doesn't mean that they practice dark psychology. In addition, it is common for people to deceive themselves about a range of issues such as their happiness, their ambition, and their health.

Deception is going to become dark any time when it is carried out with an indifferent or negative intention towards the victim. Dark deception is an understanding that the truth is not going to serve the deceptive aims of the deceiver. The deceiver is going to take the truth and either ignore, hide, or change it in favor of a version of events that suits their purpose a little bit better. Those who employ dark deception mean to do it as a way to harm, rather than to help. They want to help out their own interests, but they don't care who gets hurt in the process.

The Deception Spectrum

Deception can happen either on a small or large scale. Many people assume that deception has to occur on a large scale in order to be important. But dark deception is present in all parts of the spectrum, and it is important to be on the lookout at all times to ensure that you are safe.

Dark deceivers will often use the smaller deceptions to help them out as well. They may start out with some of these small deceptions in order to test out the victim and to condition that victim to believe the larger lies the deceiver uses later on.

Smaller deceptions can also be carried out with the goal of undermining the trust the victim has in their own powers of reason and logic. If the manipulator is able to deceive the victim over a smaller issue, and the victim starts to question what is happening, the victim may conclude that their suspicion is irrational, and they are not able to trust their own judgment. Most people will start to conclude that it is their own judgment that is at fault here, rather than entertaining the idea that someone else is deceiving them over some issue that seems so small. Of course, the dark deceiver is aware of this trust that people generally have and they will try to exploit it.

A dark deceiver can also work with a large scale deception as well. One of the largest deceptions that they can use is to convince someone that you are someone else. Not in terms of just a personality trait or some other small detail. A true deceiver can even hide their entire identity. They will hide their date of birth, their name, and everything else. This is done in order to help push forward the goals or the agenda of the manipulator.

Deceptive Topics

Everyone has heard the saying "Money is the root of all evil." This may seem like an exaggeration, but money can often be the root of a variety of deceptions. Deception and money more often than not cross paths. Some people are going to deceive in the hopes of attaining money; others will do it to hide their money, and so much more. Because money shows up as a topic so often when it comes to deception, we are going to take a look at it now.

Take a look at a professional beggar. These individuals are going to try to get money from the public, even though they have plenty of their own. These beggars are going to use a few different dark psychological principles in order to get the money they want from their innocent victims. Such beggars are even willing to put some injuries on their bodies in order to look more desperate.

Personal marital status is another area where people are going to deceive. Sometimes, a person may try to hide their married background in the hopes of seducing a new victim. This could be for sexual or financial reasons. There are even other people who have multiple wives that are spread out across the world, wives who have no idea about each other. This deception type has become even harder with the beginning of the Internet and the ability to check in on people through social media. These deceivers can manage more than one wife from each other through many different means.

There are some people who may appear to be falsely married when they are not. A married couple is one that is often seen as more trustworthy compared to one that is not married. The dark manipulator is aware of this idea and may choose to use it for their own end goals. Some people may try to have a pretend marriage to help with taxes and insurance.

One of the most common deception types with this is when the deceiver creates a fictional dead wife or husband in order to gain the sympathy of those around them and often their money.

A deceiver may also try to hide their own criminal background. This is because it is hard to be trusted, either personally or professionally, if you have committed certain crimes. Many manipulators feel like they can use deception in order to hide any socially unacceptable or abnormal feelings that they have. This can stop the victim from being alerted to the person they are dealing with until it is way too late.

For example, a dark manipulator may decide that they only want to use their victim for sex. But they know that if they focus on this topic, it is going to be a red flag and hard for them to get what they want. They then decide to deceive the victim. They may overtly lie and then imply that their true intention here is commitment and love. The victim is going to fall for this deception, the exploitation from that manipulator is done, and then the victim is the one harmed by the deception.

In a romantic relationship, the manipulator is often going to hide their true intentions. Deceptive actions and words are going to leave the victim feeling that the other person is exactly what they were looking for at that moment in time. The reason that this happens is that the manipulator is able to identify someone who is vulnerable and then probe into their needs and weak points. The manipulator is then able to use this information and then cloak themselves so they appear to be something they aren't. This is a common beginning with the manipulator that can turn into more long-term manipulations that the victim isn't aware of.

Deceptive Tactics

There are many different deceptive tactics that the manipulator is able to use at their disposal. Remember that this deception is the process of hiding information from the victim in order to reach their overall goals. There are four categories of tactics that fall into deception, and any given deception is likely to involve a blend of each of them, which can make it even harder for the victim to figure out what is going on.

The first deceptive tactic that can be used is lying. This is the first technique that the manipulator is going to choose as soon as they know that the victim is susceptible to lies and has trouble figuring out the truth. This is often because the victim is someone who trusts others. Or the manipulator may have worked on this victim for some time so that they lower their guard. The manipulator is also able to find ways to hide up the lies and then explain the discrepancies if the victim starts to notice.

Any deception that occurs with lying is likely to occur in a way that is very subtle and is thought out ahead of time. A deceiver is going to embed their lie into some information that is truthful. For example, the manipulator would start out with a story that is about ninety percent true and ten percent false. Because it sounds legitimate and most of the story can be proven as true, the victim will think the whole story is true.

Implying is another form of deception. Implying is when the manipulator is going to suggest something false is true rather than boldly stating it. If the manipulator wants to deceive a victim about how much money they have, then they could either lie or imply about it. A lie would be something like "Oh I'm a successful guy. I've made a lot of money," even though the manipulator knows this information is not true. But when they imply they are rich, they may say something like "it's so stressful trying to handle things with my accountant. Trying to get my tax bill down takes a lot of my time." The manipulator has acted and spoken in a way that makes the other person think they are wealthy, but they never state it.

Omission is another option for the deceiver. This is a failure to mention something, usually a fact that is pretty important, that is true. Omission doesn't use a falsehood in order to cover the truth like the other two options. Instead, this one is going to ignore the truth or just leave it out. Often this piece of information is important for the victim to know about in order to make an informed decision. The manipulator would leave this out to protect themselves and ensure that the victim didn't have all the information.

One way that the deceiver can use omission is to create their own emotional fence with that situation. This is a tactic where the manipulator implies that a particular period of their life, or some particular topic, is painful or uncomfortable for them to discuss. The victim, feeling bad and wanting to be considerate, will avoid bringing up this topic. This gives the manipulator a chance to avoid the truth while still making the victim feel guilty when they try to bring up that painful topic.

And the final form of deception is going to be the most elaborate, and often criminal, form. This is known as fraud. Instead of the deceiver simply lying about something from the past, this kind of deceit is going to have false stories, documents, and some other evidence in order to back up whatever their lie says. The deceiver is going to use these things in a subtle way. They would never say something like "I'm a doctor; take a look at my certificate!"

Instead, they will use some subtle displays to show off to the victim. They will try to steer away from being too pushy with their fraudulent claims because they know that doing this will make the victim feel that something is wrong with the situation.

Fraud is becoming more common than ever because of the Internet. Deceivers can often work with some professional software in order to make documents that look pretty realistic, no matter what type of document they need. This can make it really hard to tell whether you are working with someone who is telling you the truth or if they are deceiving you.

When this dark deception starts to enter the realm of fraudulence, it can be a bad sign. It shows that the deceiver is dangerous and they are committed to sticking with that dark psychology. They are risking serious criminal charges to do this kind of manipulation, and they are confident that they are able to do this without anyone really noticing it at all.

CHAPTER 9:

How Brainwashing Can Be a Part of Dark Psychology

The next topic we are going to explore is known as brainwashing. If you talk to someone and ask them what they think brainwashing is, they may reply that they do know because this is a topic that many people have heard about at some time. But most people don't have a full understanding of how this kind of mind control can work. And if you are trying to fight off someone using dark psychology, then you must make sure that you really understand this topic.

Brainwashing is going to be the slow process of taking the ideas that a victim has about their identity and their beliefs and then replacing these with new ideas, ones that are going to suit the purpose of the manipulator. Brainwashing can occur in a narrow and a wide context. For example, a brainwasher could use the techniques in order to control one person, or they could use those techniques in order to control the minds of a larger group all at once.

The Process of Brainwashing

The starting point of brainwashing is going to be the social circumstances and the mental state of the victim. This is going to be the foundation for the rest of the process, and if the manipulator is not able to figure this part out, then the brainwashing session just won't be successful. Brainwashing is not a process that is going to work out for everyone. It is going to require a good identification of a person who is looking for something or someone who has a void they are trying to fill.

This brings us to an important point. Who is the ideal victim for a brainwasher? People who have had their existing reality shaken up because of some recent events are some great targets for brainwashers. If you have lost someone you are really close to or had another dramatic or traumatic event in your life, then you may be more susceptible to brainwashing.

Once the brainwasher has found their victim, either through the Internet or in person, the process of brainwashing is able to begin. Contrary to the popular image you may have in your mind about a brainwasher, this person is often going to come across as someone who is rational, friendly, and calm. Someone who seems to have their lives together in a way the victim wishes they could have their own. Imagine how it would feel if you were homeless and a celebrity you admired befriended you. This is often how the process of meeting the brainwasher is going to feel for the victim.

The brainwasher is going to get to work right away. The first step for them is to create a level of rapport and trust between them and the victim. This is going to be done with superficial and deep similarities. The superficial similarities could involve some surface level preferences, something like enjoying the same food or sport as the other person.

They will then move on to a deeper level of rapport, some that could involve a deeper shared experience that they had in the past. The brainwasher will most likely fake these, in a convincing manner, in order to create these bonds. So, if the victim shares with the brainwasher that they lost a close relative in the past, then the brainwasher is all of a sudden going to have a story that is similar to share with the victim.

This false connection and warmth emotionally is not the only thing that is going to occur. The brainwasher wants to cement that new bond as quickly as possible. It is not uncommon for them to provide favors and gifts to their victim. They could send then a gadget or some other item they may find useful. They may treat the victim to a meal. The point of doing this is to create a sense of gratitude and indebtedness from the victim to that brainwasher. This is going to soften up a lot of the resistance that the victim may experience.

After the resistance has been stripped away a little bit, the next step is going to be a sort of utopian presentation. This is going to involve the brainwasher slowly and increasingly offering a solution to any and all problems that the victim previously opened up about. This is not going to be a big hard push or sell. Rather, the brainwasher knows how to do this in an offhand and casual way to make sure they don't deal with any negative experiences by pressing the victim. This solution is always going to be the personality, ideology, or cult that the brainwasher is working to make the victim convert too.

When these steps are done properly, the initial stages that we have discussed are going to leave the victim wanting more. The victim is going to want more information and more understanding of the solution that the brainwasher hints at. The brainwasher may even withhold some of this information in the beginning, treating it as something that the victim needs to do some work to attain. The point of doing this is to push some motivation on the victim in order to seek out and accept the information they are eventually going to hear.

After the victim has had some time being spoon-fed snippets of this belief system, and they have shown they will respond well to them, the brainwasher is going to be careful in order to reveal the right information at the right time. This is a concept that is called a gradual revelation or milk before meat. It is basically going to include the presentation of an easy to accept idea before the really controversial idea is revealed.

For example, if the brainwasher is trying to convert the victim over to religious terrorism, they would not just start out with the terrorism part. They may initially start focusing on the fact that God loves the victim, something that the victim is likely to accept. The more objectionable ideas, such as God wants you to blow yourself up, are ones that are saved until much later in the process. Once the victim has accepted that last part, then this brainwashing session is at a point of no return.

At this point, you may be curious as to why the victim is still engaging with the brainwasher, especially when these more objectionable ideas start to become apparent. There are three main reasons:

- The vulnerable victim has been worked on by the brainwasher. They feel a strong sense of liking the brainwasher, and they want to get the approval of the brainwasher.

- The victim has invested some time, and in some cases, money, in the process up to this point. This is often known as the sunk cost fallacy. The victim is going to feel like it is a bad idea to throw away all the hard work and money they have put into the process as well.

- During this process, the brainwasher has been amassing a lot of sensitive and secretive information on the victim. The brainwasher is often willing to hold this information over the victim to keep the victim on the right path.

The Impact of Brainwashing

The above analysis that we did about the process of brainwashing is going to show how severe this technique can be. It is basically changing the beliefs and the inner identity of the victim, and this can be a big deal. Sure, the manipulator is going to get what they want out of the process, but the victim is going to lose out on their real identity and often gets so far into the process that they aren't sure what went wrong.

There are a lot of different impacts that will come with brainwashing after the process is completed. The first one is a loss of identity. A feature of many ideologies and cults is that the people who go through the initiation process are given a new name. This helps the psyche of the person to completely detach from whatever their old identity is. They can believe things and even do things they never would have done in the past because that old person they were no longer exists. When this process is carried out the proper way, it can leave a victim feeling like all the parts of their old identity are no longer real or permanent and that they have woken up from a nightmare.

Post-traumatic stress disorder, or PTSD, can sometimes be a hallmark of those who managed to escape or who are rescued from a situation where they were brainwashed. The victims of these brainwashing endeavors are going to show some of the same psychological and physical signs as war veterans who were right in the battle. The severity of this traumatic aftermath shows that this type of process, of the manipulator getting more control over the victim, could harm the victim as much as if they went to war.

Brainwashing is something that can have a lasting impact. There are plenty of examples of individuals who were rescued, or who managed to escape, from their brainwashing situation, who then went back to that situation of their own free will. Even when they were able to leave the brainwashing and controlling environment they were in, the legacy that came with that process was done so well and runs so deep in their mind that the victim actually wants to return to it. This just shows the power of using this brainwashing process and how much a manipulator could gain when using this kind of process.

CHAPTER 10:

Understanding the Dark Triad and What It Means

Now we need to take a look at the dark triad. This is a very important concept because it is going to help tie together some of the other aspects that we have discussed Dark Psychology. The name "dark triad" may sound like something that comes from a horror movie, but it is actually a legitimate psychological concept that is well recognized.

The dark triad is nothing more than an identification system for the three most destructive and harmful psychological personality traits a person can have. This chapter will take some time to detail each of the traits, including narcissism, psychopathy, and Machiavellianism. Let's take a look at each part and see what it means when it comes to dark psychology.

What Is Machiavellianism?

The first aspect of the Dark Triad that we will discuss is known as Machiavellianism. This aspect gets its name from the political philosopher known as Machiavelli. In his classical work "The Prince," the ideas, principles, and tactics that are used by those who seek to influence others are outlined. But how exactly does a Machiavellian person come across?

The hallmarks of this trait include a willingness to focus on your self-interest all the time, an understanding of the importance of your image, the perception of appearance, and even the ruthless exercise of power and cruelty rather than using mercy or compassion.

To keep it simple, people who have this trait are ones who always have a strategy when they approach life. The consequences and any ramifications about any action are going to be thought out and then assessed in terms of how they are going to impact the one who is carrying them out. The Machiavellian approach to the world is summed up with a simple question: "How will this action benefit me, and how will my public perception be impacted as a result?"

Machiavellian people are going to be masters of doing what is going to personally serve them well, while still being able to maintain the good public image that they want. This allows the manipulator to do what they want, while still getting people around them to still like them.

What Is Psychopathy?

The net aspect that we can discuss is psychopathy. This is going to refer to a psychological condition that involves a superficial charm, impulsivity, and a lack of commonly held human emotions, such as remorse and empathy. Someone who exhibits enough of these traits can be known as a psychopath. These individuals are seen as some of the most dangerous people because they are able to hide their true intentions, while still causing a lot of trouble.

People often associate the word "psychopath" with an image of someone who is mad and wields a machete. The reality is different, and this can make it more deadly. A true psychopath is more likely to be that charming and handsome stranger who is able to win over their victim before they ruin those victims' lives in the process.

Interestingly, some of the top people in business score high on psychopathy personality tests. But as time goes on, it is becoming more common to see psychopathy as more of a problem to the victim and to society rather than an issue in the psychopath's own life. Psychopaths are able to get to the top of anything that they choose because they don't have to worry about some of the compassionate indecision that other humans are going to experience.

What Is Narcissism?

The third aspect of the Dark Triad that we need to explore is narcissism. This is often thought of as the idea that a person loves themselves too much. This is close but quite the right definition for someone who is a narcissist. You can have self-love without being considered a narcissist.

Someone who is considered a narcissist is likely to have a range of traits that are there. They will have an excessively inflated self-worth, such as seeing that their life is extra special and one of the most important lives in all of history. If this has been inflated enough, they may see that they are the very most important in the whole world.

In the mind of a narcissist, they are not only special, but they are superior to everyone else. They consider themselves to be a better species of person, higher than what normal people would be. And because a narcissist believes this way, their behaviors are going to change. The behavior that you see in a narcissist is going to reflect the self-worth that the person has.

Some of the outward signs or manifestations of this aspect would include the inability of the person to accept any dissent or criticism of any kind. Even if they feel that someone is trying to criticize them, they are going to have a hard time dealing with this. This kind of person also feels the need to have others agree with them all the time and they like to be flattered. If you are around someone who seems to always have a need for constant praise, recognition, and approval, and if they seem to organize their lives in order to give them constant access to those who will fill this need, then it is likely that you are dealing with someone who is a narcissist.

These three aspects are going to come together to form the Dark Triad. When one person has all of these three traits in them, it can be a hard task to stay away and not get pulled into whatever plan they have. Being on the lookout for these can make a big difference in how much control you have in your own personal life.

CHAPTER 11:

How the Dark Triad Can Be Applied

The last chapter spent some time looking at the various concepts of the Dark Triad, along with the three traits that are going to form the basis of this fundamental part of dark psychology. It is important that we not only understand the three parts of the Triad, but also the different ways that it is able to manifest itself in actual behavior. Let's take a look at the behaviors that can show this in each of the three Triad areas.

Machiavellian Actions

We already discussed how a Machiavellian person is like a political schemer who is very concerned with how the public sees them. They are almost concerned with that as much as they are with their pursuit of self-interest above everything else. So, how is a Machiavellian person going to behave? This can be hard to recognize because these kinds of people are, in their nature, adept at being able to hide all their true intentions from public scrutiny. However, there are a few different signals that you can see when you are dealing with a Machiavellian person.

First off, these people are going to have a very clear distinction between what they are and how they come across when they are out in public. For example, there are a lot of cases where a serial murderer was able to get away with the crimes for a very long time. And the main reason for this is because their outward image is so far removed from what people would imagine a murderer to be like.

A good example of this could be a religious leader. This person would spend time running their congregation, spend time doing some charity work, and seem like they always help regular people. But then on the side, they will commit horrific acts of violence. The public actions of this person are the masks that hide the private side away from scrutiny for a very long time.

Of course, there are examples of this distinction in areas that aren't as extreme as serial murder. There are many talks where the leaders in the field of business were able to ruthlessly cut jobs in order to get profits, without worrying about the people it would hurt. And these bosses, if they are really talented with the work, are able to act like they are behaving in this manner because it is a necessity, rather than just because they want more money.

Another hallmark that you will run into with Machiavellianism is a willingness to exploit other people. Let's keep with the idea of someone who is in an office and just started there. Someone who isn't a Machiavellian would look around that office and see that there is a room of different co-workers that they could get to know. But a newcomer who is a Machiavellian would see each person in front of them as another resource to exploit or use. Rather than seeing these people as fellow human beings, the Machiavellian individual would see weaknesses and other things to exploit when it works for them.

Another principle of Machiavellianism that comes from "The Prince" is the idea that the person will only keep their promise or their word when doing so will serve their own self-interest. Many people believe that a Machiavellian person is someone who isn't trustworthy, but this isn't quite right. If it is going to serve their own interests to keep their word, such as when they want to build up trust with their victim, then they will keep their word. And in many cases, when this type of person isn't able to keep their word, they will be able to do it in a way that can make them appear noble and even praiseworthy in the process, leaving them in a good light, even when they decide not to keep with the promise.

And the final hallmark that shows up for this kind of person is the ability to instill fear in others around them. This idea comes directly from "The Prince" which is going to urge a person to be both loved and feared at the same time. If it is not possible for the person to be both, then the book states that it is better to be feared than loved. This concept of the desirability of being feared and loved at the same time is directly related to the trait of splitting up the private and the public perception. The perfect Machiavellian is then able to inspire obedience and fear in the people who are most likely to claim to feel love stronger than fear as a result.

The Psychopathic Actions

In addition to some of the Machiavellian actions that we talked about above, there also need to be some actions that are considered psychopathic. Unless you have some training as a psychotherapist with an intimate access to a person, it can be hard to recognize them as a psychopath on the basis of theoretical knowledge. Since this is not likely, it is important that you are able to recognize some of the outward signs of psychopathy.

Charm is a very common outward behavior of a psychopathic person. It is going to be more of a superficial charm and never a deep or a genuine charm. If you think about someone who is genuinely charming, you would be able to pinpoint that they have a very positive personality that was under this display of behavior. This is not something that you are going to see when a psychopath is trying to be charming.

Psychopaths have the ability to show all the signs of charm, including an interest in those around them, an apparent warmth, and physical attractiveness. But the inward motivation to these displays is going to be a red flag. Psychopaths are only using charm in order to get a certain result. They see that if they present charm to someone, that person will feel good and the manipulator can use that to their own advantage. Remember that charm, just like everything else the psychopath does, is going to be calculated and shallow. There isn't going to be any depth of feeling behind the behavior.

Another sign of a psychopath is lying. Of course, lying is not enough to place someone in the category of a psychopath, but when it is combined with other signs, it can be a problem. A psychopath will find that lying is very natural, and they can do it in a very convincing manner. They also aren't going to show any signs of lying simply because they don't have an emotional attachment or any feelings of excitement, guilt, or shame about the lies that they tell. In the mind of a psychopath, lying is just "doing what is needed at the time," nothing more and nothing less.

A lack of remorse is another feature that is going to show up with a psychopath. Many people who have committed crimes, such as murder, would show a sense of shame or guilt over what they do. But a psychopath is not able to feel remorse at all. They are able to do these actions and these crimes without any feelings about it at all. Linked to this is a lack of guilt. Most humans are going to feel at least a little guilty when they go against a moral norm. But psychopaths are not going to think in terms of what is right and what is wrong. They look at things in terms of what is useful and what is not useful to them. Remorse and guilt don't fit into this at all.

A psychopath may also have a lack of impulse control. Most people are born with internal controls that will help them not act rashly in most cases. But a psychopath will not have these mechanisms. If a psychopath sees an opportunity they want to exploit, they are going to do it without a second thought. This can make them very effective when it comes to running a business or even in the military, but it can cause issues when it comes to rash decisions that could be criminal.

Psychopaths are often incapable of empathy. They may be able to fake it if it suits their goals, but they do not have real empathy at all. Other humans are just there to provide something of value to the psychopath and nothing more. If the psychopath sees that there is something bad that is happening to another person, they would just wonder how this affects me or if they could use that to their advantage. It would never be a feeling of empathy towards that person.

Narcissistic Actions

An early sign that can show up with a narcissist is fantasies and even daydreams about immense levels of status and power. Many narcissists will report that they had fantasies of being adored and worshipped even when they were children. While many non-narcissistic people may have this kind of daydream on occasion, the narcissist will feel that they deserve this elevation and praise because it is their basic right. And the fact that there are times when they are not being revered or worshipped is seen as a personal affront to these people.

The belief that "I am better than most people. They are not worthy of me. I am above them" is something that most narcissists will feel. Yes, there are times when humans are going to have an inflated sense of self-image, such as after a big achievement. But a narcissist will view praise and flattery as something that they should get all of the time, no matter what circumstances are going on around them.

The inflated sense of self-worth that the narcissist experiences internally can show up outwardly as well. This can show up in two ways. They will always have a need for praise and agreement, and they will absolutely despise any form of rejection or criticism. The agreement from others and all the praise are like oxygen for the ego of the narcissist, and they just can't make it through the day without this. If the people around them are not praising the narcissist, things can turn ugly.

An example of this is a dictator who is in a hermit state. These types of people are going to demand worship from the ones they have power over, asking for the people to build statues in their likeness and to get complete acceptance and obedience. When one of the people disagree or does an act of dissent, it is going to be met with a brutal and quick punishment.

Sadism

Sadism may not be one of the aspects of the Dark Triad, but it is still something necessary to add into this. Modern researchers into psychology have proposed that the dark triad is in fact composed of four parts and that a sadistic personality disorder should be added to this. Sadism is sometimes the hardest personality trait to understand here because it is often the least relatable out of all of them.

All of us can point out times in our lives when maybe our personality was a little bit narcissistic, psychopathic, or fit with Machiavellianism. But sadism is kind of an alien thought, and most people find that this is something that is hard to rationally understand.

Sadism is when the person derives some sort of pleasure from the suffering of others. This could add in a new and worrying dimension to the preexisting traits that we have talked about above. If the Machiavellian leader wanted to cause others to suffer, they would not regret it. But if they were a sadist as well, they would enjoy that suffering. They would actually get some sort of pleasure out of the brutal acts that occur.

The feature that is going to set sadism apart from some of the other aspects of dark psychology is the fact that it is all about cruelty. And this cruelty is just there to provide pleasure for the one using it. It is not there to serve a larger aim. It is not there for some control for the manipulator. Sadists just want to cause the suffering of others because it is entertaining for them and they enjoy watching it, and nothing else.

Often sadism is going to show up with some of the other forms of the Dark Triad that we discussed above. But it adds in another terrifying part to the mix that can make it hard for the victim to gain control again. Recognizing the signs early on is one of the best ways to keep yourself safe and to ensure that you are not taken advantage of when someone is using the Dark Triad against you.

CHAPTER 12:

Seduction With the Use of Dark Psychology

Seduction and sexual conquest are sometimes common features of dark psychology. In fact, they will show up so often that we are going to devote this chapter to them and how they work. This is an important topic to discuss because all of us have been, or know someone who has been seduced by someone else who used these dark psychological principles.

The human sex drive can be a very powerful urge and not being able to fulfill it can sometimes lead to unhappiness, worry, and stress in the person's life. On the other side of things, some of the most famous historical figures are known for their frequent and full fulfillment of sexual urges. For example, emperors and kings have often been afforded the finest women as their reward just because of their status.

One example that is very famous is the powerful seducer King Henry the 8th from England. His appetite for women was so strong that he decided to create a new religion in his country so that he could change his wife and marry any woman that he chose. He also exercised utter control over all the wives he had, and many of them were beheaded when they didn't satisfy his needs or help him meet his goals any longer.

This begs the question: Is all seduction a form of dark psychological seduction? Of course not! Yes, all seduction is going to involve the perusal of the other person. Those who don't have the skills of dark manipulation will do this in a clumsy manner. This is shown in some of the popular romantic comedies that come out, where the clumsy guy keeps making mistakes when they try to pursue the girl.

But a dark seducer is going to be someone who knows what they want and they know how to get it. They will go after the other person in order to fulfill their own personal needs, and often they don't really care how the other person feels about it. They can be charming and they are not going to be clumsy at all, and they always know the right thing to say and do.

Why Do People Choose Dark Psychological Seduction?

One question that people will have is: Why would someone want to choose this path for attraction? Is it not a better idea to go on some dates and court someone in an honest manner?

A dark seducer doesn't really want to get into a relationship, at least not into the boring stuff with it. They want to just get certain things out of the area of romance. They don't really care about the other person because they know they can use the techniques of dark psychology to find another partner later on if this one goes south later on. This allows them to approach life, and the relationship, with a non-needy and carefree mindset. If the seducer does decide to settle down with someone later on, they are going to be able to do it without feeling like they rushed or settled into the first relationship to get what they want.

So, how is a dark seducer have so much success and influence within the world of dating? It is because they understand the dark psychology principles and they have the right skills in order to execute these principles.

One of the key advantages that the users of dark psychology will have over their rivals, especially in the world of dating, is that they understand the human mind, almost like a secret weapon. While others may feel like the human mind is impossible to understand, the dark seducer is able to read it like a book and get the information that they want from it.

Someone who works on the principles behind dark psychology in the dating world may find that it is really going to change their dating experiences when compared to their past efforts. They will have a feeling of confidence and control, rather than feeling doubtful, needy, and insecure.

Sure, it may seem kind of mean. The dark seducer is able to jump from one partner to another, using each one in the manner that matters most to the seducer. And there are people who are harmed in this process, especially the ones who are looking for more of a long-term relationship, or those who are looking for more out of it.

But a dark seducer is only interested in what matters to them and nothing else. They can read the mind of their victim and be the exact person that victim wants. But they only do this to get their foot in the door and get what they want. As soon as the victim isn't meeting the needs of the seducer, then the seducer will move on.

Where Does Dark Seduction Begin?

Now that we have an idea of the basics of dark seduction, it is time to move into some of the steps of how this seduction can work. Most dark seducers are going to have a guiding approach that is going to motivate their efforts. They will also have tactics that are going to come from their philosophy. Let's take a look at some of the different philosophies that are there that a dark seducer may choose to use.

One approach is the deployment of a process that is rigid and structured. These seducers feel that they have mapped out how the sequence of attraction should be in great detail and they may have a process that seems like it is from a flowchart. They want their seduction process to be replicable and predictable. These systems not only work for the dark seducer but can work for others who understand these systems and learn how to implement them in the proper manner.

These seducers are going to use a series of stages in their process. They will try to get the target to go through a range of emotions. This range is designed by the seducer to fit their own needs. They will move them through emotions such as interest, attraction, and then excitement. These seducers will see the whole process as a series of checkpoints that they need to pass through to help them reach their goals.

The strength of this method is that it gives the dark seducer a feeling of certainty because they know the exact steps to take each time. They won't have any surprises that come up during the seduction, and it kind of becomes routine and habitual for the seducer. The biggest problem with this is that it doesn't take into account that sometimes people are going to be unpredictable and won't go along with the structured emotional program that the seducer planned out.

Another option is the natural approach. This approach is going to involve the dark seducer cultivating a genuine emotional state internal to the seducer and then expressing them freely to the one they are working to seduce. An example of this is when a person who uses this is likely to spend some time trying to understand their own emotions and then try to perfect these. They are then going to express these to others. The philosophy behind this one is that "I can't make others feel good until I can feel good."

You can also work with hypnotic and Neuro-Linguistic Programming (NLP) seduction. NLP is a combination of neurological processes, language, and behavior. This is kind of a subset of dark seduction. Unlike the structured seduction that we talked about before or even the natural version, NLP and hypnotic seduction are going to involve triggering specific emotional states in the victim and then linking these back to the seducer.

Let's look at an example of this. The NLP approach to seduction is going to involve allowing a person to explore their own intense positive emotions. The seducer may even try to get more of those emotions out. Then, they will work to anchor these to the seducer. That way, when the victim sees the seducer, they will naturally feel an intense physical pleasure, even though they may not know why that happens.

Hypnotic seduction is another option to work with, but it can be a difficult one to work with on a regular basis. This is because few things are going to make someone suspicious about a seducer than the odd techniques that come with NLP. The other seduction types are going to seem somewhat normal to the victim, but hypnotic seduction doesn't seem this way. However, there are some who will respond to it.

Dark seduction can allow the seducer the ability to get exactly what they want out of the relationship. It can sometimes be used by those who are not looking to take advantage of others, but who are open about what they are doing and just use the techniques to give them more confidence and avoid a boring relationship. But there are plenty of dark seducers who use it as a way to use the other person, with no care about how it is going to affect the other person at all. Either way, it is still important to be on the lookout for this kind of behavior so that you don't end up getting into a relationship that is bad for you or isn't what you are looking for from the other person.

CHAPTER 13:

The Techniques to Make Dark Seduction Work

We spent some time in the last chapter exploring what dark seduction is about and why someone may choose to use this kind of seduction to get what they want out of a relationship. And now that we know a bit more about the guiding principles that come behind these approaches to seduction, it is time to learn some of the techniques that the dark seducer can use to make dark seduction work for them.

The first approach that we will look at is known as the indirect approach. One mistake that you may see in conventional dating is that one or both parties will offer an icebreaker, one that is usually unappealing and cheesy, when they try to introduce themselves to someone new. They may say something like "You look pretty," "Nice eyes," or "Good song, right?"

Why are these icebreakers so bad? It is likely that the victim of your seduction has heard these countless times, and as soon as they hear them, they will be turned off and not want to talk to you at all. When the seducer uses such a bad line, it often leaves the impression that they are unappealing and bland, and no one wants to waste their time on a relationship with that kind of person.

With the indirect opener, the seducer is throwing in a breath of fresh air compared to the opening lines we talked about before. An indirect opener is going to be an icebreaker that will start the social interaction but won't convey any sexual intent. Often it is going to be posed as an "intriguing question." A good example of this would be when the seducer asks something like "Settle this for me or my buddies over there – do men or women lie more?" This is a different way to open up and talk with the other person and can start up a new conversation. And it shows the victim that the seducer is very interesting and is interested in a good conversation.

These indirect openers have the advantage of eliminating the possibility of rejection. The person who uses this kind of opener is not really offering themselves to the victim of the seduction. It is basically impossible to reject something that wasn't even offered, so it takes that part out of the equation.

Another technique to use with dark seduction is social proof. People who are popular are going to be more attractive compared to those who aren't. It is a human instinct to assume that if another person is liked by a lot of people, then there must be something that makes that person likable.

Social proof is an example of showing is more powerful than telling. Many people will try to talk about their success or their popularity, but this isn't a good idea. It is going to seem like you are bragging and can be a big turnoff to the other person. It is better to simply make sure that you are at a table or near others who are interesting. This is going to convey your social value, without seeming like you are showing off in the process.

Of course, social proof can be used for devious purposes. Think about a psychological seducer who is at a club or a bar. They see a girl that they want to seduce. Rather than directly approaching this person, they will decide to approach someone else and start a conversation with them, before moving over to their original target. This can remove the idea that the seducer is lonely, and it can sometimes spark a little jealousy that works in advantage to the seducer.

You can also work with a frame of leading to help with dark seduction. Many times you will find that the people you meet are happy to be led. Indecisiveness is one of the least attractive qualities in others. If you are able to show that you are decisive, you can automatically get the attention of others.

There are several ways that the dark seducer can show their decisiveness and that they have the ability to lead. Some of these could be physically moving around a venue, making the suggestion that it is time to change venues and not being scared to disagree with what someone else has said. Many men try to be indecisive around their victim because they don't' want to come off as weak. This is going to work against them. A dark seducer knows that they need to be decisive if they want to have any chance with the other person.

In addition to some of the techniques that we have talked about above, there are some seducers who are able to harness some of the other dark psychology traits, such as the use of psychopathy, in order to reach their romantic goals. For example, one trademark of psychopathy is the ability of the seducer not to feel any fear when they interact with other people.

Many times a man or a woman is going to be paralyzed by fear, especially when there is a chance for rejection by someone they are interested in. A dark seducer is not going to have this fear because they just don't understand the fear at all. Even if you are not a dark manipulator and you don't regularly use dark seduction, you can use this idea. A psychological seducer is going to learn, over time, that it is better to be the one who tried and failed rather than the one who didn't have any confidence to try in the first place.

Why Are Dark Seducers So Dangerous?

A dark seducer can be a formidable foe. They know exactly how to get the other person, their victim, to fall in love with them. But the problem comes with the fact that the dark seducer really isn't in love with the other person. There is something that the dark seducer wants out of the relationship. This could be companionship because they don't like to be alone, sex, or something else. But they are usually not looking for love at all.

As soon as the victim of this seduction doesn't provide the thing that their seducer wants, the seducer is going to leave. So, if the victim starts to feel that they are being used and withholds sex from the seducer, the seducer will simply leave the relationship and move on to their next victim.

The seducer has no worries about the other partner in the relationship. A true seducer is only going to see the other person as a tool, something that helps the seducer get the pleasure that they want. As soon as that tool stops doing the job that it's supposed to, the seducer will move on to find a new person to do the work for them.

A dark seducer may move quickly between one relationship to the next, or they may even stay in a relationship for a long time. It all depends on the situation and how long the seducer is able to keep the victim under their control. Some victims stand up for themselves pretty quickly. The longer the victim is under the control of the dark seducer, the harder it is for them to leave.

This doesn't mean that the dark seducer has learned how to love their victim. It simply means that the dark seducer has become used to the way that things are, and they will use their powers and their mind control techniques in order to keep the victim right where they are.

How to Avoid Dark Seduction

It is important for you to be aware of dark seduction. While some men may choose to use some of the ideas of dark seduction in order to help them gain some confidence, avoid some issues with their fear of rejection, and make it easier for them to meet women, there are many that will use these techniques because they don't really care about the other person at all. They have specific goals that they want to reach in the relationship, and they will get there, no matter who gets hurt in the process.

If you do end up getting into one of these relationships, it can be devastating. The dark manipulator is really skilled at using the dark seduction techniques to get what they want. They will find a victim who is vulnerable, and they will present the right solution that the victim needs at that time. For example, they may find a victim who just got out of a major relationship, and they will step in to feel the need of that victim to not be lonely any longer.

The seducer is going to be charming, fun, and the perfect person for that victim. The victim may feel like they have found their soulmate, but the seducer is just there to get what they want out of the relationship. Sure, it may last for some time, but as soon as the victim is no longer meeting the needs of the seducer, the seducer will be gone.

This will leave the victim hurt and broken. They may have overly trusted the seducer (because the seducer is skilled at reading the victim and knew exactly what to do and say to gain that trust and get what they want), and now they are broken. They may go through depression and anxiety and even have trouble trusting others in the future.

Because of all these negatives that come with dark seduction, it is important to watch out for the signs. If you run into dark seduction with a narcissist or with a psychopath, it is even more important to watch for the signs. These individuals are not there to care about what the other person wants. They simply look out for themselves, they feel that they deserve what they want, and they don't have the capacity to care about how it is going to harm the other person.

Due to the way that the relationship was started, including the romance, attraction, the mutual feeling that you found a soulmate (all created by the seducer to get what they want), when things start to take a lot of wrong turns, it is likely to be too late for you, the victim, to walk away. This can be especially true if you went into that particular picture without a good idea of what you wanted in the relationship. Without this clear picture, you would not have the determination to walk away from that relationship when it didn't meet your expectations.

This is why you must always make sure that you know what you want to get out of the relationship before one begins. This will help you be prepared if the relationship becomes something else because you will be able to see when it is going away from your chosen course. You will give yourself a chance to see it for what it is before you damage your self-worth so much where you will stay in that relationship and accept the bad treatment.

This can be hard. Many times we feel that we need a relationship like we are not worth anything unless we are in a relationship with someone else. Then, when we are not in a relationship, we are going to feel like something is missing, and we jump into the first relationship that comes available. This is where the issues will start.

Before you jump into the next relationship, it is important to take some time to soul search. Remember that there is nothing wrong with not being in a relationship all the time. Taking some time for yourself and really exploring where you are at that time in your life and what you would like to happen in your next relationship can make a difference.

This gives you a good idea of what kind of relationship you want to be in. You won't just jump into the next relationship because you are needy or because you worry about being alone. You will have specific goals in mind, and if you feel the relationship isn't going in the right direction, you will be able to step out before the dark seducer gets too deep and tries to take control over you.

The first thing that you should do here is to start with some deep thinking and even some soul-searching and decide on the details of the relationship that you are looking to enjoy at that time in your life. Describe what you want out of the other person in this partnership. Describe how you want to feel in this relationship. Set out some clear boundaries and then make sure that you understand why you have these boundaries.

CHAPTER 14:

Case Studies of Dark Psychology

This guidebook has taken some time to talk about the different aspects of dark psychology, something that is a very powerful tool for a manipulator to use. But now it is time to take a look at some of the case studies, or examples, of how these different methods were used in real life. Remember that the case studies that are shown in this chapter are some of the more severe examples of dark psychology that have occurred during human history to help give a good idea of how it works.

Ted Bundy: Final Testimony

Ted Bundy is perhaps one of the most notorious serial killers in all of history. One of the more fascinating aspects of his story is the amount of material that was published about him and the crimes he committed and how willing Bundy was to give interviews. With many other high-profile criminals, the hype level and intrigue are often going to outweigh the crime that was committed. But this is certainly not the case with Bundy.

There is still no confirmed total number of murders that are linked to Ted Bundy. He was only charged with 30, but he has hinted that the total is probably closer to 100. No one knows for sure and many analysts feel that Bundy even doesn't know how many people he killed. There are a lot of details that relate to the crimes that Bundy committed, and this has helped explore more about the world of psychopathic serial killers, the methods they used, and some of their motivations for doing it.

Bundy really understood the power of perception and the public image. It is undisputed that many of the people who encountered him, even during the time when he was performing these murders, found him to be attractive and charming. This is a hallmark of psychopaths who are able to show off an outward appearance of desirability and charm without any inner truth to what they are showing. The emotional coldness and detachment of men like Bundy become clear when you stop and consider that a human being was able to inspire attraction and comfort in his victim's moments before killing them in some of the worst crimes in history.

Hitler

There are many parallels that can be drawn between some of the political ideas of Machiavelli and the political career that Adolf Hitler took. The argument can be made in many cases that Hitler is sometimes the best illustration of what the modern Machiavellian leader will look like.

One of the first similarities that are there between Hitler and Machiavelli is the idea that peace should only be seen as a little break in a war that never ends. Hitler was very devoted to conquest and planned to use his Third Reich to take over the whole world. Hitler was a good example of a ceaseless warrior ruler. Machiavelli was also an advocate of creating and then changing reality to sort a predetermined political aim. Infamously, one of the core doctrines that was found with Hitler was the persecution and the extermination of much of the German Jewish population. The main event that made it easier for Hitler to work on this is the false flag operation that was known as the Reichstag Fire.

Another key idea that comes with Machiavelli's political thought is that power is a worthy end goal all by its one. No matter what methods are then used by the individual to get and hold onto the power, they can be justified with the blueprint of how a leader needs to behave. Hitler is a good example of this concept in action. Hitler was a genius at manipulating the current political system while also working on the minds and the hearts of the people of his country.

And one of the most important and apparent links that is out there between these two is the idea that "it is better to be loved and feared, but if that is not possible, feared rather than loved." It is pretty easy when looking through textbooks to see the devotion, worship, and love that Hitler was able to inspire on the German people at that time. Yes, we have now painted Hitler as the epitome of evil, but at that time, Hitler was adept at getting responses of love and fear out of his people. Just take a look at some of the videos of the speeches that Hitler used and you will see this in action.

Rasputin: Dark Psychology or Black Magic?

You can't go through case studies on dark psychology without taking into account Rasputin and everything that this monk represents. Rasputin is an interesting figure because the type of power that he wielded in this field has echoed way into the future and it even inspired the aspects of many charismatic influencers that came around later on.

Rasputin was a spiritual figure who was able to use his powers to gain some influence over the Russian rulers of that time. He was able to project an intoxicating mix of sensuality and piousness that appealed to almost any side of a person that Rasputin wanted to work with. Those who may have been more inclined to follow religion were very impressed by the powers of healing the monk seemed to have. But those who enjoyed the sensual pleasures of the world were also able to find things to admire in the character of Rasputin. The most influential part of Rasputin's character was the fact that he was able to be an angel and a devil at the same time.

Many parts of the influence of Rasputin can be found in modern-day users of hypnosis. Rasputin was one of the most infamous, and perhaps earliest, figures to induce something similar to a trancelike state of suggestibility on the minds of any victim he chose.

What were these healing and hypnotic powers that were rumored to belong to Rasputin? It is believed that he was able to induce in his victims some deep feelings of relaxation, ease, and calm. He is well known for his abilities to ease the aches and pains anyone in the Russian family dealt with at that time. This helped to add some more to his mystique and really increased the amount of influence that he had on everyone near him.

Rasputin also did many things that are now common in covert emotional manipulation. One of the reasons that Rasputin had such a big impact on those around him is that it never seemed like he was trying to control the victims. Instead, he was able to come across as someone who had an unexplainable power that people would just succumb to. These are all hallmarks of cover emotional manipulation as it is used in modern times.

The case study of Rasputin is relevant when it comes to those who are learning more about charismatic influence. Like Rasputin, many modern-day dark psychological manipulators are able to attract followers, often because there is a perception out there that these manipulators possess a secret or some special knowledge.

This principle was way more effective back in Rasputin's time. The world was not used to this form of deception like it is today, and rational and science were less developed. This help to give some more credence to the idea that Rasputin was a divine as well as a powerful person. Students of this dark psychology are going to be able to draw a lot of parallels between the power of a supernatural portrayal and similar charismatic leaders of the modern world who would feign spirituality in order to gain the control and influence that they wanted.

The link that is present between sexual expression and psychological power is very clear in the story of Rasputin. Similar to what many others did throughout history, Rasputin was able to leverage his dark influence into a life of decadent indulgence and even promiscuity. It is not a coincidence that many cult leaders, no matter where they are found or practicing throughout the world, are often found enjoying their choice of followers in any manner that they choose. While Rasputin may be an infamous example of this, he is not the first person to ever use these techniques.

Con Artists

Many of us have heard about the different things that con artists can do. They seem to have powers of being able to persuade anyone to act in a certain way that benefits them the most. And while some people on the outside can tell that something is going on, those who are in the middle of the trap from that con artists are often going to follow along blindly.

A good example of what a con artist can do is a Ponzi scheme. This name comes from Charles Ponzi, a man who was able to conduct a large-scale fraudulent investment scheme. One of the striking features of this Ponzi scheme was the fact that Charles was willing to use the power of projection and portrayal of his own confidence to help him get out of any sticky situation. For example, there is a story about how Charles once had a group of angry investors who show up at his place. Rather than panicking at the situation, Charles remained calm and collected and was able to use his own tranquil demeanor in order to calm down the mob.

Gregor MacGregor is another example of this, and he was one of the earliest examples of someone selling things that don't actually exist to others. If you have heard stories of a con artist who sold something like the Brooklyn Bridge or the Eiffel Tower to naïve folks who had wealth, then the con artist got the idea from Gregor MacGregor.

MacGregor was able to do this because he insisted that he was nobility, but he came from some islands that didn't actually exist. He would recruit people who had wealth to help fund expeditions over to these islands, all while knowing that these islands weren't there. The reason that there is sometimes a lot of interest in MacGregor is that he was so convincing to these victims, and he knew how to work with their psyches and egos, that even after they tried to visit these nonexistent islands, they would still defend MacGregor to the press. This just shows how strong and advanced the covert manipulation abilities of MacGregor were at the time.

Con artists can show us a lot of lessons in dark psychology. These con artists have the ability to psychologically influence other people, often to the amazement of other people. The case of Ponzi shows the importance of working on a victim that is vulnerable, then exploiting that vulnerability ruthlessly, and then doing this in a way that doesn't betray a hesitation or a doubt. Ponzi is a great example of how you are able to increase how likely it is that a fraud will work out simply by the manipulator being confident, having control, and appearing like they are not worried ever. It is also a good example of showing that some of the best con artists can keep these scams going for decades before they are exposed.

MacGregor is able to offer an almost amusing insight into the power of taking the ego of someone and then using it against them. Despite the fact that the wealthy investors had been exploited financially and had wasted their time going to these fake islands, and even the fact that they looked stupid in the process, they still chose to defend MacGregor to the public.

What are the lessons we can take away from this in terms of dark psychology? If a victim who has a high opinion of themselves and a high status is found, they are unlikely to admit when they were conned or when they were tricked. It is likely that they are not even going to admit what really happened to those events, even to themselves. This is a good example of how the narcissism of a person can be used against them.

These are just a few of the examples of how dark psychology has been used throughout history. There are many more examples, but this shows how dark psychology works and that it is an actual thing, not just something you hear about or read about!

CHAPTER 15:

Common Cons Worldwide and the Dark Psychology Behind Them

As we had mentioned before, con artists are a great example of dark psychology at work. As such, we thought you might enjoy a chapter detailing a number of famous cons practiced across the planet. This can keep you out of trouble when you run into these scams yourself, and can also teach you a little of the dark psychology behind the con. Some of them are only mildly malicious, but others are quite horrible. We hope this will help to explain a little the mindset behind these dark persuaders so that you may be better equipped to avoid them in your future. Before we go into this list, let's discuss a little how con artists most often use dark persuasion so effectively.

Embarrassment

Con artists know that a majority of folks will NOT report the incident, as they will feel embarrassed at having been manipulated by a scammer. If it happens to you, you should report it, because we can guarantee that you are probably not the only one and it might not stop for a very long time without your help.

Mirroring Your Body Language

Con artists know that by mirroring your body language, you are more likely to like and trust them. Be sure to watch out for this technique in order to help protect yourself.

Dress for Success

Con artists know that you are more likely to trust someone who is well-dressed than you are to trust someone who looks like they just came in off the street. They will take advantage of this. Watch out when someone very well-dressed starts treating you like a best friend, especially if they are talking about new business opportunities. If you do decide to do business, it can wait, and there is nothing wrong with insisting on a background check.

Appear Trustworthy

Con artists will buy you drinks, tell you stories that make them seem more down to earth, and, if you aren't careful, they will win your trust. A con doesn't always occur in the space of an evening, so even if you have known someone for a month or two, you should still be careful where money is concerned. Anyone whom you barely know that asks "Do you want to make some money?" should be viewed with suspicion at the very least.

Get You Talking About Yourself

As dark manipulators, con artists know that people like you more if you get them to talk about themselves. They also know that this gives them information which they can use against you in order to get what they want. Pay attention to their body language and remember the background check advice that we gave you. It gets you information, it's legal, and you can throw it away once you've protected yourself by checking. It's not popular advice, but it is good advice.

Target You When You Are Vulnerable

Dark manipulators know when you are vulnerable and likely to make bad decisions. Con artists are among the best of them. If you've recently lost someone or lost your job, and someone has popped into your life that you seem to be spending a suspicious amount of money around, be careful. This might be the kind of 'friend' that you'll never see again once the money is gone.

Play on Your Greed

The scams that con artists like to employ the most are those that play on your greed. They usually involve buying items or investing in something that is going to have an unrealistic turnaround time and profit. Be especially wary if there is a time limit or it's a 'one-time offer.' If it sounds too good to be true, it probably is.

Now that we have mentioned the base tactics employed, here are some examples of real-life cons to give you a glimpse into this branch of dark manipulation:

1. **"Your Hotel is Full"** - This may be familiar to some of those out there with a fondness for travel. If you have never experienced this ruse before, a taxi driver will get you in the car and when they hear the name of the hotel that you are going to, they will then advise you that this hotel is full/overbooked that night and offer to take you somewhere nice where you will be able to get a room. Many weary travelers have fallen for this one, providing unscrupulous business for the taxi driver and the hotel which is owned by one of his friends or family members. This can be easily avoided by insisting that the driver take you to your hotel, by calling your hotel, or by leaving the unscrupulous cabby's vehicle immediately to find yourself a more honest driver.

2. **The Petition** - This one is popular in Paris, but occurs in many places around the world. When entering an area of interest to tourists, you'll notice a number of people going around with clipboards. They will come up to you and advise that they are rallying for a particular cause and ask

you to sign a petition. Once signed, they will then insist that you have to donate and they will get 'offended' if you resist. Many people will pay to avoid a scene, or to avoid being viewed as someone who cares for a cause but is not willing to help. Avoid the clipboards altogether, as they are only after your cash.

3. **Renting a Vacation Apartment** - This one is particularly nasty and occurs in many places across the globe. A con artist posing as a tourist will rent a property with stolen cards, only to then begin advertising the property on the Internet so that they can collect as many cash deposits as possible before fleeing the scene. By setting the availability date of the property to be 'at the end of the month' and giving out keys to help sell the con, they end up with a lot of money and a vast amount of time so that they can be long gone when the duped people start arriving. If it's too good to be true, it probably is. Make a paper trail and never pay a cash deposit.

4. **"I'm Making a Video!"** - One story we've heard was a con involving a woman who went into a popular expensive clothing store in another city, claiming that she was a music

producer. She told them that she was making a video and that the store could advertise their items if they were willing to donate clothing for the band members to wear in the videos. As she had had the place scoped out well beforehand, she knew who could and could not make that sort of decision, and was able to procure some very expensive clothing at someone else's expense.

5. **Art student** - A very popular scam in Europe, tourists will find themselves approached by someone friendly who claims to be an artist working their way through art school. They will be asked to see the art on display, and only find out too late that they have paid 2-4 times the cost of the copy print they have just purchased.

6. **Your Grandson is in Jail (or the Hospital)** - This one is truly horrible. Many con artists, scammers, and other dark manipulators will arm themselves very well to get what they want from you. Information is something they covet. Finding out your name from your mail or from bills in the trash, things only get worse from there. For a time, there were reports of dark manipulators contacting elderly targets and telling them that their grandchild was in jail and needed

money wired for a bond or worse, that they were in the hospital far away and needed someone to get money to them. Using the love for a family member is truly vicious, and helps you understand that some of these people will stop at nothing to get what they want.

7. **Versace Manager Needs Gas** - Everyone has had someone come up to them at a gas station and ask for money but one con artist was a bit more prepared. Dressed in expensive clothes and claiming to work for Versace, this individual asked for gasoline, and even showed the targets fabric and clothing samples in the process to make them feel that this was just a person down on their luck. Reportedly, some people made loans to this person for 20, 50, and even 100 euros. Trust, but verify. You can be a good Samaritan and still be careful.

8. **Dead Husband's Debt** - Another very horrible scam perpetrated largely on the elderly. Con artists will review obituaries in order to find out the names of the recently deceased so that they may contact the widow or widower. They will then proceed to tell them that their spouse owed a sum of money and attempt to collect on this while the

victim is in a vulnerable emotional state. Dark manipulators like to catch us when we are imbalanced and, for many of them, nothing is sacred. If you ever experience someone contacting you like this, be sure to go straight to the police.

9. **Broken Meter** - Another staple when traveling to a new city or a new country, the old 'broken meter' trick has fleeced many a victim. The scenario is simple. Your taxi arrives, you get in, and are advised that the meter is broken as the cabby starts to pull out of the pick-up zone. Once you reach your destination, the price has been doubled or tripled and they will threaten to call the police if you don't pay. Let them. In this information age that we live in, you can easily map a route from the airport on your smartphone and demonstrate the distance.

The difficult part, however, is that this is very popular in many foreign countries where you may not speak the local language. The best that you can do is make sure that the meter is running before you leave and, if not, insist on another ride.

10. **Bird Poop Clean-up** – This is a common street scam. Imagine that you are walking and someone comes up to you and points out what looks very much like bird poop on your shoulder. This person immediately pulls out a handkerchief and offers to help you out of this embarrassing situation by cleaning off the offensive item. You thank them and leave, only to find that they also cleaned out your wallet and smartphone. If something similar to this happens to you while on vacation, don't let anyone clean your clothing, simply thank them and go into the nearest bathroom to do it yourself.

11. **Reshingle Your Roof Scam** - In 2016, there were a number of reports of another scam targeting the elderly. People going door-to-door offering roof repair services. These shady characters would charm the individual they met at the door into hiring them, and then ask for lump sums of cash in order to obtain materials. One pair of men were arrested for this scam, but many more have tried and succeeded in this dark manipulation. As we mentioned before, always create a paper trail!

12. **Friendship Bracelet** - This is a tourist scam that occurs in a number of locations. An individual will approach a tourist and simply place a 'friendship style' woven bracelet on their arm, tying or weaving it quickly into place. They will then demand payment for the work rendered, which tourists will often pay just to avoid a scene. This is also done with small sketches or cut-out silhouettes of couples. When approached, the best defense is to walk away quickly as they can be very persuasive.

13. **Group Photo Camera Theft** - An individual approaches a group of tourists offering to take a group photo if someone has a camera. Once everyone has gotten in place, the camera has already been handed off or the individual simply runs away. They then pass it to a friend so that you cannot get it back, and so they won't have it if the police do happen to be around. Try to get other tourists to help if you would like a picture. It isn't foolproof, but the odds are better in your favor for avoiding this sort of scam.

14. **Fake Hotel Credit Card Check** - Some dark persuaders have a con where they call someone in their hotel room in the middle of the night in order to advise that their

card has been declined and they will need to provide another number. Tourists who had enjoyed rather a lot during their time in the city, and were perhaps not in the best state of mind when they received the call, were all too happy to provide this information so that they could continue their party or simply go back to sleep. In the morning, of course, they would find out that they had been duped. Never provide your credit card information over the phone. In a case like this, a simple trip downstairs or dialing '0' could have cleared things up rather quickly.

15. **Streetfighting Lure** - Imagine that you are in a foreign country and you come across a group of people beating an old man or woman. Jumping in to help, you hear a smartphone making the 'shutter' sound of a photo being taken. You've just fallen victim to a dark manipulation. The entire group, the 'victims' included, will now threaten to give the photo to the police and claim that you were assaulting the very people that you tried to help. Terrified of police in a foreign country, many people will simply pay to get away. Avoid fighting in foreign countries if at all possible. Learning the emergency number for the police

before you arrive can save you a lot of trouble (and perhaps a trip to the hospital).

16. **Marrakesh Snake Charmers** - In Marrakesh, you should be careful around the snake charmers. One common tactic employed to fleece tourists is that the charmer will walk up and quickly put a small snake on your neck, expecting to be paid. Tourists generally don't mind, as this is entertainment and their job; however, if the amount is not to their liking, then these same tourists sometimes find themselves surrounded by a number of angry people who are in on the con. This can result in pickpocketing, potential violence or, at the very least, a lighter wallet as they will do their best to 'surround you out of view.' Of course, not all snake charmers do this, but be on the lookout and don't let anyone put anything on you just in case.

17. **New Orleans Shoes** - This one is apparently quite popular and not very complex. An individual at the bar will bet you 10$ that they can tell you where you got your shoes. If the bet is accepted, they will simply say "You got them on your feet in New Orleans." The problem arises if you decide

you don't want to pay and they happen to have a number of friends present.

18. **Pigeons in Venice -** In this little number, a man or woman will approach you and press a small sack of grain into your hand. They then whistle and the pigeons come flying in for the grain. They offer to take a picture for you if you will hand them your camera or smartphone but, if you do not wish to pay the rather high price for your pictures, they will threaten to keep the camera. As mentioned before, dark manipulators can make a situation appear magical and wonderful until it's time to give them what they want.

19. **Dancing Mickey and Minnie -** This old classic is actually very fun to watch, you can sometimes see it in Rome. You will walk by someone who is dancing next to a boom box type stereo and dancing there as well are cartoon characters. The story is preposterous, but people still fall for it. The dancing person will claim that there are special magnets on the little characters that respond to design of standard speakers (of course, it's just fishing line. The paper characters 'dance' as the bass vibrations bounce the fishing line). These are actually fun souvenirs, but only if you can

get them for a single euro. They are not worth the 5 euros you'll be asked.

20. **Bangkok Gem Scam** - This one is a little more complicated, but what occurs is that a tourist is routed from a popular site, typically by being told that it is a holiday. They are given a promise that there are other sites they can see free and sent along their way, typically after the individual re-routing them has garnered information that they can use (typically things like where they are from, how long they are staying, and what kind of work that they do). They inform the next person that the victim will meet them. When the victim arrives at the temple that they have been sent to, the next part of the con begins. They will meet someone who will begin telling them that the government is closing down a scheme that allows people to purchase jewelry and ship it to their home duty-free, making sure to mention that this is the 'last day' that they can do this.

Usually the victim's new 'friend' will take them to one or more temples where they will happen to meet more people, sometimes local or Westerners, who corroborate the man's story. This leads up to a trip to a jewelry store where the victim is told he can get a better rate on the jewelry with the purchase of gold to trade for the gems (which helps in money laundering and prevents a stop-payment). The gems are packaged and 'shipped' to their home address, preventing an independent valuation, ensuring when the victim gets home that if the gems even arrive, they will be of a much lesser value than expected.

The world of dark manipulators is rather frightening indeed, no? These are just the ones who are after your money, but many will use dark psychology to play with your feelings, turn you against allies, and more. We hope that this information will help you to be better prepared if a manipulator of this sort comes into your life. We hope, of course, that this never happens but, if so, then you will have a better idea how they operate and will thus be much less likely to fall for their games. Sometimes that is the best that we can do. In our next chapter, we have gathered together information on another useful set of subjects. Micro expressions, which are a set of 7 emotional cues that can be read in someone's facial expressions, and a list of nonverbal cues, some of which you will know already and some of which you may not have already been aware of. We've compiled them together in one place so that you can study and practice them in your free time in order to better prepare for attempts to use such information against you. Remember, knowledge is power, so learn and practice reading these telltale signs that the body gives, which can inform you if someone is saying one thing but quite possibly meaning another. Let's proceed now to the next chapter. We think that you will find it most useful!

CHAPTER 16:

Micro Expressions and Body Language – A Basic Primer

Imagine if you could 'read' body language to an extent where you knew exactly what someone was expressing, despite the actual words that they were telling you. This is actually something you that you can do to an extent. Let's talk about micro expressions. Popularized largely by a show entitled 'Lie to Me', which told about the fictional life of Dr. Cal Lightman, 'Lie to Me' was the story of a behavioral specialist who could tell if someone was lying based on facial tics and tells which would let the doctor know if someone was lying or otherwise engaged in deceit.

The science from the show is surprisingly 90% accurate but, while they cannot tell you if someone is actually lying, they can give you a very good idea if someone is experiencing emotions contrary to the story that they are telling. So, how accurate is the science? It's accurate enough that it is taught to the FBI and the U.S. Secret Service. First discovered in 1966 by Dr. Isaacs and Dr. Haggard, micro expressions gained popularity later with the research of Dr. Paul Ekman. Reviewing many stills of psychiatric sessions, Dr. Ekman was able to discern 7 different emotions that were present, despite the language or culture of the individual being reviewed. Fascinating, no? We're going to go a little into micro expressions and then further into common body language vs. culturally influenced body language in order to better enable you to deal with practitioners of dark psychology.

these are actually just indicators of the presence of feelings rather than actual proof of deceit, it is still a fascinating science which can be useful to you – 7 different universal factors that you can see clearly on someone's face if you know what you are looking for. Even a seasoned dark psychologist can't hide the emotions if you know where to look.

The 7 emotional factors (which show regardless of your linguistic or cultural background) are as follows:

Happiness - Lip-corners are turned up. Wrinkling (crow's feet) at the sides of the eyes are present, along with a raising of the cheeks.

Anger - Lips are pressed tightly together. A widening of the eyes and lowering of the eyebrows into the middle of the forehead occur as well.

Sadness - Lip-corners are turned down. Eyebrows angled, close together and raised.

Fear - A widening of the eyes and raising of the eyebrows occurring with slow opening and widening of the mouth. Upper eyelids will be pulled up/in.

Surprise - Similar to fear, an open mouth with a widening of the eyes (the pupils will dilate as well) and raised eyebrows.

Disgust - Wrinkling of the nose and a raised upper lip, with lips loosely displayed.

Contempt - Head goes slightly back and one side of the lips is raised.

These are just some quick examples in what is a very rich subject. Any of the books by Dr. Paul Ekman are good for research on this, as well as a quick Google. A number of the sites display facial examples in order to help you to familiarize yourself with the different expressions in order to apply them for your own use, and there are even a number of video courses on this for you to better learn.

Aside from micro expressions, many body language expressions can be useful to learn when determining if someone may be sending you mixed messages, either consciously or subconsciously.

Let's review some nonverbal cues that you see daily and talk about their most common meanings. Learning these cues can help you to better determine if the words that someone is saying to you match what their body language is telling you. Remember, nonverbal cues are not a 100% foolproof of reading intentions, but they can be very, very useful to you. Some have been mentioned before, but we have collected a list in this chapter in order to place them with other cues that you may also look for. Be sure to look for as many of these cues in the next few days to see how common they are. They are an excellent tool in avoiding becoming a victim of dark psychology.

Nonverbal Cues Associated with Sitting:

Nonverbal cue: Someone sitting with legs crossed, foot kicking slightly up and down.

Often indicates: This one we've all done. It typically indicates boredom and a little impatience (although the latter is not guaranteed, as many of us do it without thinking). Not generally something to worry about unless someone claims to have great interest in what you are saying at the time.

Nonverbal cue: Sitting with legs apart comfortably.

Often indicates: Generally something you'll see men do most of the time. This is indicative that the person is relaxed and comfortable with your presence.

Nonverbal cue: Their ankles are locked together while sitting.

Often indicates: This one typically indicates a state of apprehension or nervousness. If combined with some of the other worry expressions here, it could mean that they have some bad news for you or are worried about your reaction to something.

Nonverbal Cues Associated with Arms:

Nonverbal cue: Arms crossed over the chest.

Often indicates: Unless it's cold out, this is typically a defensive posture. You won't see it so often with figures of authority who tend to display arms comfortably at their sides, or perhaps with a hand in one pocket to indicate ease.

Nonverbal cue: Complete stillness of the arms in conversation.

Often indicates: This is one to watch for, as stillness of the arms can indicate purposeful masking of body language or tenseness at the very least. Proceed with caution.

Nonverbal cue: The gripping of one's own arm.

Often indicates: Gripping one's own arms is a gesture of self-comfort with typically negative connotations. You'll see this one a lot when people are waiting in a government office to renew a license and the wait is long, on airplanes from those with a fear of flying, or quite commonly, in doctors' offices.

Nonverbal cue: Their arms and hands are held low in front of them, with hands clasped.

Often indicates: This is a position of defense and can indicate that the subject is feeling vulnerable or otherwise insecure about their position in the conversation. Keep in mind that dark psychology practitioners are also aware of this and may adopt this stance to appear more vulnerable. You see this pose adopted often when people are asking for help.

Nonverbal Expressions Associated with Fingers and Hand Gestures:

Nonverbal cue: They have their hand resting on their cheek.

Often indicates: This can indicate that someone is thinking or perhaps evaluating the situation.

Nonverbal cue: Touching the nose or scratching the nose.

Often indicates: This can indicate disbelief or, in some cases, may indicate that the person is deceiving you. Watch for how they do it. Usually, a genuine scratch is going to be quick and efficient. If it is occurring a lot and it's not cold season, then this may be a nonverbal cue to watch for.

Nonverbal cue: Someone is rubbing one eye while you are speaking.

Often indicates: This is another indicator that someone may not believe what you are saying. Take the weather in consideration and, if the rubbing of the eye seems a bit fishy, then note it to yourself.

Nonverbal cue: Someone approaches with their hands clasped behind their back.

Often indicates: This can indicate frustration, irritation, and anger in many cases. It is sometimes adopted as a domination posture in the workplace, as well as a way of showing aggression.

Nonverbal cue: Someone has their head resting in one hand and their eyes looking down.

Often indicates: This one typically just indicates that the subject is bored.

Nonverbal cue: Someone is sitting with their hands clasped behind their head and with their legs crossed.

Often indicates: Confidence, superiority.

Nonverbal cue: Someone is steepling their fingers while speaking to you.

Often indicates: This is typically a gesture of authority where the person that you are speaking with feels they are the dominant presence.

Nonverbal cue: Someone presents open palms when they see you.

Often indicates: This is a gesture meant to show sincerity and to inspire openness in a conversation. It is also a way of communicating symbolically 'I have no weapons in my hands, you can trust me.'

Nonverbal cue: Someone pinches the bridge of their nose, closing their eyes momentarily.

Often indicates: This generally indicates that someone is responding negatively to the subject at hand.

Nonverbal cue: Someone is drumming their fingers on the table or tapping.

Often indicates: This is something we've all seen and merely indicative of impatience.

Nonverbal cue: Someone is playing with their hair.

Often indicates: If this behavior is not in an atmosphere conducive to flirting, then it can indicate that the person is feeling insecure.

Nonverbal cue: Someone is moving around excessively.

Often indicates: If someone you are speaking with is playing with their pencil, tapping their feet, or playing in their chair, basically any excessive movement as if distracted, is a common indicator of impatience.

Nonverbal cue: Someone is stroking their chin.

Often indicates: This is commonly associated as an evaluation gesture and indicates that someone is coming to a decision.

Nonverbal Gestures of the Head:

Nonverbal cue: Someone quickly tilts their head slightly during a conversation.

Often indicates: This is an indicator that what you have just said or something they have noticed in the environment has suddenly gotten their attention. It is always a good thing to notice when leading a conversation or ascertaining motives.

Nonverbal cue: Lowering of the head in conversation.

Often indicates: There are a number of meanings to this depending on a few factors. For instance, a quick lowering of the head is a mini-nod, indicative of an agreement or feigned agreement. If eye contact is maintained, it can be a sign of flirtation or an indication of distrust, depending on the context. If lowering the head so that the chin is covering the neck, then it is a defensive gesture. It can also indicate frustration or exhaustion, although, in such cases, it is often followed with a sigh.

Nonverbal cue: Their head is perfectly still while speaking to you.

Often indicates: This can indicate that the person is serious or feels they are speaking from a position dominant/in authority of you. This can also be indicative of anger or potential violence.

Miscellaneous Nonverbal Cues

Nonverbal cue: Invading personal space.

Often indicates: Typically a distance of one foot is reserved for family and friends so if someone you barely know is doing this, you should be on the lookout. Four feet is the typical comfort distance for personal space in most countries.

Nonverbal cue: Body-language mirroring.

Often indicates: Be careful. The person might be doing this unconsciously, as mirrored body language tends to put the recipient at ease; however, this can also be a conscious attempt to put you in the same state. Be wary of this one.

Nonverbal cue: Object barriers.

Often indicates: This is done most often subconsciously and represents the act of putting a barrier between them and yourself. This is typically a means of avoiding showing your insecurities to someone. The next time you are in a bar or a similar public venue, take a look around and you'll see people doing it, usually with their glasses clasped in both hands in front of them.

Now that we have gone a through a number of nonverbal cues, it is worth noting that there are some cues that you may never see due to cultural differences. For instance, closer proximity is considered aggressive in Japan. Constant eye contact also makes people very uncomfortable, whereas in Spanish and Arabic cultures, NOT maintaining a lot of eye contact is considered very disrespectful. For the majority of the nonverbal cues here, however, you shouldn't have any problems, just be sure to do a little research if you like to travel so that you don't misinterpret a cue if you intend to go somewhere exotic.

Now that we have given you a larger sampling of the information that you need, you will want to practice it. As mentioned at the beginning of this chapter, take a week looking for nonverbal cues, such as you have read in this chapter, to see how many of them that you can identify. You will find a number of them readily in the workplace and at social venues that you frequent. Use this information to better arm yourself for dealing with dark psychology. Knowing them may not guarantee that you will be immune to being manipulated, surely not, but not knowing them will most certainly guarantee to make you less likely to notice them when you should be on your guard. Arm yourself as best you can with this information, it's the good stuff!

CHAPTER 17:

Reality Denial 101 - Gas Lighting Techniques

We spoke in Chapter 3 about reality denial and how dark manipulators can use it to make their victim seem as though they were crazy. In our previous chapter, we went through micro expressions and described a number of nonverbal cues that you can keep the knowledge of at your disposal. In this chapter, we would like to go over a number of reality denial techniques that have been grouped together under the term 'Gas lighting.' This particular form of manipulation can be quite insidious and difficult to protect yourself from, but we can introduce you to some common methods and suggest to you some possible means of defense in order to combat this dark art.

Gas lighting is popularly used by the Dark Triad, most commonly in the following ways:

- Machiavellians - Machiavellians will typically employ Gas lighting in order to protect a particular self-image that they would like to portray. On Internet forums or social media such as Facebook, this most commonly includes taking arguments out of context, or looking for the weakest aspect of an argument in order to attack the other person's credibility. They often spend a lot of time in political forums as this is an emotional subject for many and therefore an easy place to get themselves the attention they crave. Typically, they offer a broad subject, a vague solution (or no solution) for, and then let people start arguing. It's trolling, but trolling in the sense that the Machiavellian is doing it in order to forward a self-image of appearing calm and rational to cultivate their self-image at the expense of the unsuspecting.

- Psychotics - Psychotic motives are much harder to place, but typically they involve self-advancement. A psychotic might seem cheerful and kind at work, for instance, and yet if they are competing with another for a promotion, they will spend a lot of their free time deciding how they can discredit the other. They will not hesitate to magnify the details of a situation in order to get a co-worker fired if that person is in their way. This lack of remorse and empathy is what makes this member of the Dark Triad so deadly. They are easily the worst of the group.

- Narcissists - Narcissists will typically employ Gas lighting in an attempt to attack anyone who they feel is arguing with them. The goal is to debilitate the individual in the eyes of others; thus, elevating the status of the Narcissist. It may also be used as simple punishment for someone who has dared to challenge their precious self-image.

So, how do you recognize when someone is attempting to use Gas lighting techniques in order to disorient you or to undermine your confidence? We've compiled some techniques here that can give you an idea of some of the more common methods. Reality denial manipulation can be quite nasty, so you will want to study these techniques so that you can recognize when dark manipulation is afoot and is pointed at YOU.

Here are some common methods employed in Gas lighting:

1. **Lying about friends to isolate you** - Dark manipulators want you isolated and, in order to do that, they need to erode your base of support. They begin dropping hints about your friends, accusing them of belittling you behind your back, not respecting you, or perhaps of having a romantic interest in the manipulator. They know which buttons to push so this can be very effective, especially if they have been using the next item on our list.

2. **They often take their time to become your best friend** - Master dark manipulators will take their time to begin tampering with your mental stability. It will likely begin with small examples from this list and then proceed to a full-on assault. Over time, it gets worse and worse and there is added confusion from the 'nice period' that came before. Watch for small examples from this list and, if you see them, take it as a warning sign.

3. **Project their feelings on to you** - Dark manipulators will often project their own feelings and insecurities on to you. A very common example in a relationship with one of these individuals is constant accusations that you might be cheating on them. You'll notice that they seem to know a lot about the subject, and this is a warning sign that can help you to see what is really going on more quickly. If you are getting accusations of this sort for no reason, then be on the alert and ask yourself why they seem to know so much about how a cheating person is likely to act.

4. **Tell you that you are imagining things** - This generally goes with the previous relationship tactic and can be indicative that they are doing something or many things behind your back. In relationships, we tend to notice when our partners experience a change in behavior. If it is easier to accuse you of having an overactive imagination than it is to explain themselves so that you don't worry, then this can be a very big warning sign to watch for as well.

5. **Lie to discredit your memory** - This is a favorite Gas lighting tactic and very easy to do. If someone sets up a day to meet, for instance, and then later tells you that they never

set that up time to meet with you, then you will find it curious at first, but likely never suspect it to be deliberate. They can also express interest in going to a concert or a movie with you and then, when the time comes, act bored or irritated at the event, later claiming that they told you that they didn't want to go to that but that you insisted. It is a tried and true technique and you should watch out for it. A good way to combat this is simply write things down or put them in your calendar immediately and discretely, so that you will know if it occurs more than once. If so, either their memory is quite poor or they may be attempting to Gas light you.

6. **Get you angry and accuse you of being crazy** - When a dark manipulator knows how to push your buttons, they will often take advantage of this to make you doubt your very sanity by using your temper. It will seem as if every quarrel consists of you yelling and frustrated, while they calmly suggest you have a drink, relax, or perhaps that you both meet another time 'when you are less irrational' or 'less crazy.' This, of course, will make you angrier, giving them an excuse to leave, and later to question whether or not your

response was appropriate (especially if followed by the silent treatment, forcing you to communicate first). If you DO have a temper, that doesn't necessarily mean that someone is taking advantage of it, but a constructive way to help determine what really occurred is to write down your version of events when you get home, and to wait to read it until the next day. That way, you can view it when you are less upset and if it is something that is occurring regularly, you will be better equipped to determine if it is an actual problem with anger, or if this person might be manipulating you towards their own ends.

7. **Mix abuse with praise or gifts** - Dark manipulators like to keep you off-balance by mixing abuse with praise. For instance, you may find yourself being complimented for something innocuous after a brutal argument, or treated to a nice dinner or event after days of silence, with the abusive behavior which was recently experienced never spoke of... as if it never happened. These mixed messages allow the manipulator to prolong their control. If someone is being abusive in the first place, it is best to disassociate with them

as soon as possible but, barring this, analyze their behavior and look for patterns from this list.

8. **They will use your children** - If you have children, dark manipulators will not hesitate to use them against you – raising the volume of their speech so that you will capitulate with their wishes, rather than let your children hear you arguing. They will also bribe children with treats and pushing your buttons so children will always associate the manipulator with ice cream and toys and you with anger and yelling. If you notice this behavior, take it for exactly what it is, blatant manipulation, and get as far away as you can from this individual. This is not the sort of thing that gets better over time.

9. **Accuse you of wasting efforts in the wrong place** – This one can occur in the home or the workplace. You will find your Manager asking, "Why are you wasting time doing this particular assignment when I needed you to do this other one?" after they clearly asked you to focus on the first. This is an attempt to bully you, an act of dominance. The only way to really combat this is to mark items on your calendar 'Priority per Boss' as they come in or, otherwise,

create a paper trail for yourself. While taxing and monotonous, this method is an effective way to defend yourself from this sort of manipulation.

10. **Turn others against you** - Gas lighters know the people who dislike you already and will resort to name dropping to this effect. "Joe knows you are lazy at work" or "Jill says you cheated on a boyfriend once." This works well with the isolation technique as suddenly not only do you not have your friends, but everyone around is an enemy. Watch out for name-dropping of this sort, as dark manipulators love to use this technique.

We hope that this list of techniques employed by dark manipulators has been of use to you. Use this information well and you'll certainly have the basics of defense at hand should you need it!

BONUS!

As an additional 'thank you' for reading this book, I want to give you another book for free. The book is:

The Simple and Powerful Word To Use to Increase Your Social Status

It's a quick read that will add a powerful tool to your psychological toolbox.

Follow the link below and you can claim the book instantly.

Click Here for Instant Access!

or go to VictorSykes.com/free-ebook

Conclusion

Thanks for making it through to the end of *Dark Psychology*. Let's hope it was informative and able to provide you with all of the tools you need to achieve your goals whatever they may be.

The next step is to be on the lookout for those who may try to use some of these techniques against you. If you are not on the lookout, a dark manipulator may be able to use these tactics against you, and you may never know.

The goal of this book is to keep you out on the lookout for the dark manipulators who may show up in your life. When you know some of the signs to watch out for and you understand dark psychology, you can protect yourself and stay safe! You are the one who should be in control over your own mind. Don't let someone else take that away from you!

Finally, if you found this book useful in any way, a review is always appreciated!

CPSIA information can be obtained
at www.ICGtesting.com
Printed in the USA
BVHW061010140121
597841BV00009B/355

9 781087 859132